The 30-minute Vegetarian

About the Author

David Scott is joint proprietor of the Everyman Bistro, one of Liverpool's most successful restaurants, which is featured in all the major wine and food guides and which, after 16 years in operation, is almost part of the fabric of the city. He is the author of eleven cookery books with a vegetarian or Eastern flavour, including classics such as *Middle Eastern Vegetarian Cookery*, *The Japanese Cookbook*, *Traditional Arab Cookery*, *The International Vegetarian*, with Jack Santa Maria, *The Vegan Diet*, with Claire Golding, and *The Gourmet Vegetarian*.

*Also available from Century Hutchinson
by David Scott*
Traditional Arab Cookery
Middle Eastern Vegetarian Cookery
Grains! Beans! Nuts!
Protein-Balanced Vegetarian Cookery
The Gourmet Vegetarian
The Vegan Diet (with Claire Golding)
Indonesian Cookery (with Surya Winata)
The International Vegetarian (with Jack Santa Maria)
A Taste of Thailand (with Kristiaan Inwood)
The Fighting Arts – Choosing the Way (with Mick Pappas)

Also by the same author
Recipes for Living
The Japanese Cookbook
Seasonal Salads (with Paddy Byrne)

OVER 200 FAST & EASY RECIPES
FOR THE HEALTHY COOK
IN A HURRY

The 30-minute Vegetarian

DAVID L. SCOTT

CENTURY
LONDON MELBOURNE AUCKLAND JOHANNESBURG

First published in 1986 by Century Hutchinson Ltd,
Brookmount House, 62–65 Chandos Place, Covent Garden,
London WC2N 4NW

Century Hutchinson Australia Pty Ltd,
PO Box 496, 16–22 Church Street, Hawthorn, Victoria 3122, Australia

Century Hutchinson New Zealand Limited
PO Box 40-086, Glenfield, Auckland 10, New Zealand

Century Hutchinson South Africa Pty Ltd,
PO Box 337, Bergvlei, 2012 South Africa

Designed by Linde Hardaker
Photographs by Ian O'Leary
Home Economist: Judy Bugg
Stylist: Carolyn Russell

Set in Linotron Trump Mediaeval by
Rowland Phototypesetting Ltd
Bury St Edmunds, Suffolk
Printed in Italy by New Interlitho

British Library Cataloguing in Publication Data

Scott, David, *1944–*
The 30 minute vegetarian: over 200 fast
and easy recipes for the healthy cook in
a hurry.
1. Vegetarian cookery
I. Title
641.5′636   TX837
ISBN 0 7126 1298 X (cased)
ISBN 0 7126 1440 0 (paper)

ACKNOWLEDGEMENTS

I would like to thank Paddy Byrne, one of my partners in
the Everyman Bistro, Liverpool, for permission to use a
number of his recipes in this book. I would also like to
thank Rita Trotter, who typed this manuscript very
accurately and quickly and at the same time checked
and unified the metric and imperial equivalents given in
the ingredients lists. My final thanks go to Century
Hutchinson, the publishers of this book. As an organiza-
tion, they are refreshingly enthusiastic and
professional

Contents

LIST OF ILLUSTRATIONS

INTRODUCTION

This book is aimed at those vegetarians with limited time or inclination to devote to cooking. Its aim is to provide a collection of recipes that offer a flexible, fast, simple and nutritious approach to vegetarian cookery. None of the recipes needs longer than 30 minutes to prepare, and many take much less.

Fresh or dried ingredients are used throughout, with the exception of canned chick peas and red beans. The recipes in the Salads chapter do not contain eggs or dairy produce – salads containing these ingredients appear in the Eggs, Cheese and Yoghurt chapter. Most of the recipes in the book are suitable for vegans; others may need a little modification.

I have concentrated on offering new ideas that will stimulate the cook's imagination into creating his or her own dishes. The origins of the recipes are varied, but because the cuisines of the Far East are renowned for their fast cooking methods several dishes have been included that come from this part of the world.

HOW TO USE THIS BOOK

All the recipes in this book are listed under conventional headings such as starters, soups, desserts and so on. Those appearing in the chapters on vegetables, grains and dairy products tend to be suitable as main courses, although a number of the salads are also quite substantial.

To plan a meal, choose one or two dishes that appeal to your personal tastes and suit the time and ingredients you have available. If you want to make two courses – say a soup and a main course, a soup and a salad, a main course and a dessert, or a salad and a starter – make sure that they dovetail with each other, so that while one is cooking the other can be prepared. As a general rule, soups and dishes containing grains and/or vegetables should be put on to cook first, and cold dishes made last. Where a finished dish is at its best chilled, use ingredients straight from the refrigerator and forgo the usual chilling time. Read the recipe right through before you start cooking and plan your method of preparation accordingly.

Alongside each recipe title preparation and cooking times are given. Underneath, the amount of 'free time' is often also given – this covers that part of the preparation and cooking time during which the dish is simmering on top of the stove or baking in the oven, and does not need to be supervised. This time can be used for preparing another dish, clearing up, laying the table and so on.

The times given assume that all the ingredients have already been assembled. Because cooking times are subjective, the times have been rounded up or down to 5-minute intervals.

THE 30-MINUTE VEGETARIAN AND A BALANCED DIET

In order to function at the optimum level the body needs protein, carbohydrates, vitamins, minerals and fats in the right combination at the right time. A vegetarian diet can successfully provide all these requirements in a natural and balanced manner. A mixed, moderate diet of fresh vegetables, grains and grain products (e.g. pasta, bulgar wheat, etc.), dairy products, pulses, fruits, nuts and seeds and unhydrogenated vegetable oils will supply all our nutritional needs. We should also avoid, where possible, refined foods since they often contain additives, saturated fats and too much sugar or salt. Overcooking also seriously reduces the nutritive value of most foods. Here is a closer look at the individual nutrient groups.

Protein

The question that often bothers people is whether a vegetarian diet will provide enough protein – they are hooked on the idea that only flesh foods can provide enough. This question is answered completely in the affirmative both in the findings of academic nutritionalists and in the active and varied lives led by practising vegetarians – men, women and children. They include many top sportsmen and sportswomen, some of whom take part in very tough endurance events such as marathon running. There is also some evidence that in cultures in which a vegetarian diet is traditional, such as the tribes of the Caucasus and the Pakistani Hunzakut, people live to a much greater age than do, say, Eskimos or Laplanders, who are dependent on a meat-rich diet.

The main sources of protein for the vegetarian are grains, pulses, green leafy vegetables, milk, cheese, yoghurt, eggs, nuts and seeds. Eaten in combination, these foods will provide enough high quality protein for almost all human requirements.

If eaten in the right combination vegetarian protein foods are also increased in biological value – which means the amount of protein they contain that can be used by the body. This is a principle called complementarity. Thus a dish containing rice and lentils supplies protein of more value than the same total weight of rice or lentils eaten on their own. This is because some of the essential amino acids from which the body makes proteins are in short supply in one of the foods but available in excess in the other, and vice versa with other amino acids.

There are many examples of complementarity, and it is a good general rule to include in each meal two of the vegetarian protein foods that complement one another. The best combinations are:

1 Milk, cheese, yoghurt and other milk products either in or with any dish containing grains, pulses, nuts or seeds.
2 Grains (either whole or as a flour product) either in or with any dish containing pulses or dairy products.

3 Pulses either in or with any dish containing grains, dairy produce or nuts and seeds.

   Green vegetables, especially eaten raw, may also make an important contribution to your protein intake since they contain complete protein of the highest biological value.

Fats

A concentrated energy source, fats contain the all-important fat-soluble vitamins A, D and E. Every fat or oil contains active (unsaturated) or inactive (saturated) acids. The active acids, called essential fatty acids (EFA), are found in their highest concentrations in vegetable oils. Saturated fats, which are linked to the risks of heart disease, high blood pressure and some cancers, occur in their highest concentrations in animal fats and some dairy products. The intake of fats of any kind should be moderate; where possible, use vegetable oils such as corn, olive, peanut, safflower, sesame, sunflower and walnut. Incidentally, cold-pressed oils and margarines contain more natural nutrients than do heat-extracted oils.

Carbohydrates

The body's main source of energy, carbohydrates are present in foods as starches and sugars. Starch is obtained from cereal grains and their products, pulses, vegetables – especially root vegetables – and nuts. The complex combination of starches and protein in these foods is a good one for people involved in manual work or sport. Naturally occurring sugars are found in fruits, honey and milk. Refined sugar, added liberally to so many foods today, should be used only moderately. It lacks every nutrient except carbohydrate, and by spoiling the appetite it tends to displace from the diet other foods containing necessary nutrients.

Vitamins and Minerals

The body cannot synthesize the vitamins and minerals it requires, and they must be supplied in the food we eat. The vitamins and minerals are an unrelated group of substances, but their functions in the body are inter-related and they are all required in the right balance. A mixed diet of grains, pulses, dairy products and vegetables – especially salads and fresh fruits – will normally provide all the vitamins and minerals we need.

Fibre

Found in unrefined cereals, fruit and vegetables, fibre is not a nutrient because it is not digested. However, because it adds bulk to food it is an essential factor in the efficient elimination of the body's waste products.

Flesh Foods

By removing flesh foods from our diets we reduce our intake of saturated fats. We also avoid consuming the chemicals fed to animals to make their flesh the right colour and degree of tenderness for the market, and at the same time contribute in a small way to the alleviation of the suffering inflicted (albeit not intentionally) on animals by modern factory farming methods.

STORE CUPBOARD

Fast food preparation needs certain essential ingredients in stock, easy to get at and easy to put away again. Here are the basic store cupboard ingredients required for the majority of the recipes in this book. Items that are best bought fresh every week are included in the weekly list at the end.

Oils Olive oil; a neutral oil (such as peanut or sunflower); sesame oil, safflower oil. Cold-pressed oils are the best, if available.

Herbs Fresh if available, otherwise dried. Oregano, mint, bay leaves, basil, thyme, rosemary, sage.

Spices Whole seeds preferably. Black pepper, cumin, coriander, cinnamon, turmeric, sea salt, white pepper, curry powder, cayenne, mustard seeds, caraway, cloves, allspice.

Vinegars Organic cider vinegar, rice wine vinegar, wine vinegar.

Flavourings Naturally fermented soya sauce (shoyu), hot pepper sauce, fresh ginger root, garlic, vegetable stock cubes, tahini, peanut butter, creamed coconut, miso, honey.

Grains and Pulses Long grain white rice, bulgar wheat, dried pasta (including egg noodles), split red lentils, couscous, canned chick peas and red beans.

Canned Goods Plum tomatoes, chick peas, red beans, sweetcorn, tomato puree.

Bottled Goods Olives, mustard, chutney.

Nuts and Seeds Sesame seeds, sunflower seeds, walnuts, almonds.

Dried Fruits Not essential, but useful.

Weekly List Natural yoghurt, lemons, cheese, fresh cream, beancurd (and tempe if available).

he dishes chosen for this chapter perfectly fill the role of hors d'oeuvres or starters, but they may also be served in combination with one another, or in some cases on their own to make interesting and colourful light meals. For instance, Fried Cheese with Olives served with Apples and Grapes in a Japanese Mustard Dressing and French bread makes a nutritious and delicious light lunch.

If you are preparing one of the starters in the conventional sense and intend to follow it with one of the other recipes in the book, plan your timetable carefully. If the other recipe requires cooking time, initiate it and then move on to making the starter. Exceptions are the two starter dishes Tropical Fruit Refresher and Apples and Grapes with Japanese Mustard Dressing. They need chilling before serving, so make them first and put them in the refrigerator until needed

Starters

Tropical Fruit Refresher

SERVES 4

A very quick, exotic starter. If the fruits suggested are
not available use others such as passion fruit, lychees
and so on

½ large pawpaw, flesh scooped out
1 large banana, peeled
2 kiwi fruit, flesh scooped out
½ pint/275 ml orange juice

garnish

4 thin slices orange

Put all the ingredients except the orange slices into a blender and liquidize
until smooth. Chill and serve in small glasses, each decorated with a slice of
orange.

PREPARATION TIME 5–10 MINUTES
CHILLING TIME 20 MINUTES

Honey Glazed Mushrooms

SERVES 4

Serve hot or cold as a starter or as an accompaniment to
other dishes

1 lb/450 g fresh button mushrooms
1 tablespoon peanut oil
1 tablespoon clear honey
2 tablespoons soya sauce

Wipe the mushrooms clean and trim the stalks level with the caps. Heat the
oil in a wok or frying pan and swirl it round so that it coats the inside of the
vessel. Add the mushrooms and stir fry for 1 minute over a medium heat.
Add the honey and soya sauce, turn the heat low, cover and cook for about 3
minutes. Uncover and cook until the mixture thickens, turning the
mushrooms in the honey and soya mixture to coat them.

PREPARATION AND COOKING TIME 10 MINUTES

Starters

Herb and Nut Salad Balls

SERVES 4

These salad balls served on a bed of lettuce make a
lovely and unusual starter

1 large apple, peeled and finely grated
1 large carrot, scrubbed and finely grated
2 oz/50 g cashew nuts, ground *or* other ground nuts such as almonds
1 tablespoon freshly chopped chives *or* spring onions, finely chopped
1 teaspoon lemon juice
small head lettuce

Thoroughly mix together by hand the apple, carrot, nuts, chives and lemon
juice. Form tablespoon-size quantities of this mixture into moderately
tight-packed balls. Wet your hands if the mixture sticks too much. Serve on
a bed of lettuce.

PREPARATION TIME 15 MINUTES

Pears with Brie Dressing

SERVES 4

There are many light fruit and cheese starters; here is a
particularly pretty one

4 tablespoons plain yoghurt
2 oz/50 g soft Brie, skin removed and diced
2 teaspoons freshly chopped chervil *or* spring onion
salt *and* black pepper to taste
2 ripe, tender pears, skinned

garnish

12 black grapes, halved and pips removed
2 teaspoons pine nuts
paprika

Combine the yoghurt, Brie and chervil in a small mixing bowl and beat well
together with a fork. Season with salt and pepper. Core the pears, slice them
lengthwise and gently stir the slices into the yoghurt mixture. Divide the
contents of the mixing bowl among 4 small plates, top with the grapes and
pine nuts and finish with a light dusting of paprika.

PREPARATION TIME 15 MINUTES

Starters

Fried Cheese with Olives

SERVES 4

In this Egyptian recipe cubes of cheese are fried (at the table if you wish) with whole olives and served sprinkled with lemon juice, accompanied by chunks of fresh, crunchy bread. French bread is particularly good. If you have a presentable frying pan transfer the pan from the stove to the table and serve the dish straight from the pan. The diners scoop the cheese and olives from the pan with pieces of bread

1 tablespoon butter
8 oz/225 g hard cheese (mature Cheddar *or*, if available, Haloumi)
cut into ½ in/1 cm cubes
12 black olives, whole *or* pitted
lemon juice

Melt the butter in a heavy frying pan and add the cheese and olives. Fry gently and turn the cheese cubes around continuously. As soon as they are hot, sprinkle them with lemon juice and serve. Do not worry if some of the cheese melts too much and the cubes lose their shape. It still tastes good scooped up in the bread.

PREPARATION AND COOKING TIME 10 MINUTES

Sharon Fruit Delight

SERVES 4

This recipe is a good starter if the rest of the meal is to be very filling. Use the fruit and orange juice straight from the refrigerator and serve the Delight as soon as you have prepared it, since it is best slightly chilled. Incidentally, Sharon is the Israeli name for a persimmon

2 persimmons, cut in half and scooped out
1 orange, peeled and chopped
2 pears, quartered and cored
orange juice to taste

Put all the ingredients into a blender. Blend until smooth, adding as much orange juice as necessary to get a medium thick texture. Transfer to individual bowls and serve immediately.

PREPARATION TIME 10 MINUTES

Starters

Coriander Mushrooms

SERVES 4

4 tablespoons olive oil
1 teaspoon coriander seeds, freshly ground
1 bay leaf
9 oz/250 g fresh white button mushrooms, stems trimmed
2 teaspoons lemon juice
salt and pepper to taste

garnish

bay leaves and lemon slices or wedges

Pour the olive oil into the pan and heat it over a medium flame. Add the ground coriander and the bay leaf. Immediately the bay leaf starts to darken tip in the mushrooms and then the lemon juice. Season with salt and pepper and cook, stirring frequently, for 3–4 minutes or until the mushrooms have a translucent look about them (achieved when the hot oil has penetrated the centre). Adjust the seasoning and transfer the contents of the pan to a serving dish or individual dishes. Garnish with bay leaves and lemon and serve.

PREPARATION AND COOKING TIME 10 MINUTES

Cashew Nut and Tofu Pâté

SERVES 6

1 tablespoon olive oil
1 small onion, finely diced
1 small clove garlic, crushed
4 oz/100 g toasted and ground cashew nuts
6 oz/175 g tofu (beancurd), drained
4 tablespoons water *or* white wine
2 tablespoons chopped parsley
sea salt to taste

Heat the oil in a shallow pan and sauté the onion and garlic until softened (about 5 minutes). Add this mixture to the nuts in a mixing bowl, then mash in the tofu. Stir in the wine, parsley and salt. Press the pâté into individual ramekins, smooth the top of the mixture and serve.

PREPARATION AND COOKING TIME 15 MINUTES

Starters

Apples and Grapes with Japanese Mustard Dressing

SERVES 4

1 teaspoon prepared English mustard *or* Japanese wasabi mustard
2 tablespoons rice vinegar *or* cider vinegar
1 tablespoon shoyu (natural soya sauce)
1–2 teaspoons sugar
8 oz/225 g eating apples, cored and cut into small chunks
juice of ½ lemon
8 oz/225 g large grapes, washed
1 teaspoon mustard seeds

Combine the mustard, vinegar and soya sauce in a small mixing bowl, add sugar to taste and stir well to dissolve the sugar. Set aside in the refrigerator. Sprinkle the apple chunks with lemon juice and set aside to chill. Cut the grapes in half and pick out the pips with the tip of a pointed knife. Lightly chill the grapes. Before serving, toss the apple chunks and grapes together in the dressing and then distribute the salad among 4 individual bowls

PREPARATION TIME 15 MINUTES
CHILLING TIME 15 MINUTES

Mushroom Pâté

SERVES 4

2 tablespoons vegetable oil
1 large onion, peeled and chopped
2 teaspoons fresh rosemary *or* 1 teaspoon dried rosemary
1 small clove garlic, crushed
12 oz/375 g mushrooms, washed and chopped
3 tablespoons wholemeal flour
1 teaspoon miso
soya sauce to taste

Heat the oil in a pan and sauté the onions, rosemary and garlic for about 5 minutes. Put the mushrooms in the pan and cook over a moderate heat for a further 5 minutes. Add the flour and cook, stirring, for a further 7–8 minutes. Put the mixture into a blender and add miso and soya sauce to taste. Beat to a smooth paste. Serve the pâté smoothed down in individual ramekins.

PREPARATION AND COOKING TIME 25 MINUTES

Starters

Fried Cheese with Olives served with Apples and Grapes in a Japanese Mustard Dressing and French bread makes a nutritious and delicious light lunch

Soups make a tasty start to a simple two-course meal or, with bread and a simple salad, a substantial meal in themselves. *From the back*: Gazpacho Soup; Clear Soup with Lemon and Beancurd; and Cream of Almond Soup

Spicy Lemon Cucumber Salad

SERVES 4

This cucumber salad is excellent as a light, refreshing starter or as a side dish. In the Far East it would be made from the small gherkin-type cucumbers sometimes available in the West from Indian grocery stores. This type of cucumber is used unpeeled and unseeded. Ordinary cucumbers are also fine for the recipe, but they need peeling and seeding

1 lb/450 g small gherkin cucumbers, finely sliced *or* 1 medium cucumber, peeled, seeded and finely sliced
1 medium onion, finely sliced
1 tablespoon salt
3 tablespoons lemon juice
¼ teaspoon cayenne (add more if you like hot food)
2 tablespoons sesame seeds
1 tablespoon sesame oil *or* peanut oil *or* sunflower seed oil

Combine the cucumber, onion and salt in a bowl and mix well together. Sit a plate on top of the mixture and weight it down with a cupful of water. Set aside for 20 minutes in the refrigerator and then drain off all the liquid that forms. Gently press the cucumber and onion to extract more liquid, which should also be discarded. Stir in the lemon juice and cayenne. Dry roast the sesame seeds until they start to jump in the pan, then add them to the bowl together with the sesame oil. Mix well and serve.

PREPARATION TIME 30 MINUTES
FREE TIME 20 MINUTES

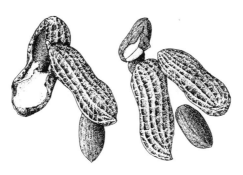

Starters

Celery with Green Pepper and Sesame Sauce

SERVES 4

2–3 sticks celery, including leaves, washed
1 large green pepper
2 tablespoons soya sauce
1 tablespoon sesame oil
1 teaspoon brown sugar

garnish

8 very thin slivers fresh root ginger
2 teaspoons sesame seeds, dry roasted

Heat a small pan of slightly salted water to boiling. Cut the celery diagonally into 2 in/5 cm lengths. Retain the leaves. Cut the pepper in half, core and seed it, cut it in half again and then cut each piece into quarters. Blanch the celery and pepper pieces in the boiling water for 30 seconds only. Remove and drain. Mix together the sesame oil, soya sauce and brown sugar. Stir this sauce into the vegetables and distribute them among 4 individual plates. Garnish each with a few chopped celery leaves, slivers of ginger root and sesame seeds.

Sweet-sour variation For a sweet-sour sauce add 1 tablespoon lemon juice to the sauce ingredients.

PREPARATION TIME 10 MINUTES

Mushroom and Vegetable Salad in Lemon Shells

SERVES 4

This Japanese-inspired starter traditionally uses white radish (daikon), but the little white turnips available in Britain in the winter and spring months are just as good

4 medium lemons, cut in half
4 oz/100 g little white turnips *or* white radish (daikon), grated
4 oz/100 g young carrots, scrubbed and grated
4 oz/100 g button mushrooms, sautéd in a little oil and chopped
2 tablespoons cider vinegar
2 teaspoons sugar
½ teaspoon salt

garnish

4 sprigs parsley

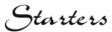

Starters

Cut around the flesh of the lemons just inside the skins and scoop out the flesh, leaving 8 empty shells. Squeeze the flesh and reserve the juice. Combine the turnip, carrot, mushrooms, vinegar, sugar and salt and 1 tablespoon of the lemon juice, and mix them well together. Divide the salad among the 8 lemon shells. Serve them in attractive bowls and garnish the tops with parsley sprigs and a few drops of lemon juice.

PREPARATION TIME 15 MINUTES

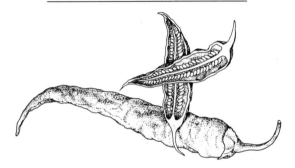

Green Apples with Sweet Hot Sauce

SERVES 4

For this recipe use crisp, slightly sweet apples such as Granny Smiths. Serving apples in this way usually causes a surprise, for people are not used to seeing them in such strange company

4 crisp green apples, cored and sliced into 6
1 teaspoon lemon juice
3 tablespoons soya sauce
4 oz/100 g white sugar
¼–½ teaspoon chilli sauce
1 tablespoon finely diced onion

Place the apple slices in a bowl of water with the lemon juice and place the bowl in the fridge to chill slightly (20 minutes). Put the soya sauce and sugar in a small pan over moderate heat and gently melt the sugar in the liquid. Pour the mixture into a small bowl and set it aside for 15 minutes to cool. Just before serving stir the chilli sauce and onion into the soya sauce and sugar mixture. Set the bowl of sauce in the centre of a serving plate, arrange the drained apple slices around it and serve. Diners dip apple slices into the sauce and eat them.

PREPARATION TIME 30 MINUTES
FREE TIME 20 MINUTES

Starters

Mezze

SERVES 4 OR MORE

Mezze are Middle Eastern hors d'oeuvres. They may be hot or cold – and either complicated and exotic or simple and quick to prepare. Here is a selection of ideas for readily available, easily made salad mezze. Choose 3 or 4 and arrange them on individual plates for each diner. Consider contrasts in colour, texture and taste when making your choice. Serve the mezze with fresh bread, wedges of lemon and a small bowl of lightly salted natural yoghurt. No fixed quantity has been given, since the amount you prepare of each mezze will depend on how many guests you have and how many mezze you wish to put on each plate. They should look delicious and tempting but shouldn't be filling – just appetizing.

Slices of onion and tomato arranged in a circle of alternating rings, garnished with chopped parsley or mint.
Wedges of cucumber.
Yoghurt, slightly salted.
Pickles: gherkins, onions or other pickled vegetables.
French beans, lightly cooked, dressed in oil and lemon juice.
Artichoke hearts or okra in olive oil.
Cottage cheese or yoghurt or both, mixed with tahini and sprinkled with cumin seeds.
Shredded, chopped or sliced raw vegetables.
Slices of hardboiled egg, dusted with cinnamon, coriander and salt.
Lemon wedges.
Radishes on ice.
Fresh dates stuffed with cottage cheese.
Fresh dates in yoghurt.
Tahini seasoned with crushed garlic and lemon juice to taste.
Ripe avocado flesh mixed with finely chopped onion and tomato, seasoned with salt and black pepper, dressed with lemon juice and served on lettuce leaves.

Starters

The soup recipes given here are very suitable for a quick two-course meal. They may be prepared in advance, and then left to cook through or to keep hot on a low simmer while you make another dish. A number of the soups, however, particularly those with longer preparation times, are quite substantial; served with bread and a simple salad they make a satisfactory meal in themselves.

The quality of many of the soups depends to some extent on the availability of a good stock. Buy the best vegetable stock cubes you can, or, if you have time to spare, make your own.

The quickest way to make stock from stock cubes or granules is to put the right amount in a blender, add the right quantity of water (use nearly boiling water from an electric kettle if the recipe requires hot stock) and pulse the machine for a few seconds

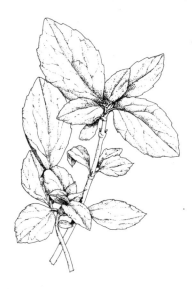

Soups

Clear Soup with Lemon and Beancurd

SERVES 4

A light and simple but tasty and visually attractive soup.
See the ginger variation below

1½ pints/850 ml clear vegetable soup stock
6 oz/175 g tofu (beancurd), cut into ½ in/1.25 cm cubes
1 lemon, thinly sliced
2 spring onions, finely chopped

Bring the stock to the boil and add the beancurd. Reduce the heat and simmer for a few minutes. Divide the soup and beancurd among 4 bowls, taking care not to crush the beancurd. Decorate each bowl with slices of lemon and spring onion. Do not crowd the bowls with ingredients. If you have too much lemon or spring onion, save it for future use.

Variation with ginger Replace the lemon slices with 2 teaspoons finely chopped root ginger.

PREPARATION AND COOKING TIME 10 MINUTES

Quick Peanut Butter Soup

SERVES 3–4

This is a very good soup, often a favourite with children

1 large onion, chopped
1 tablespoon vegetable oil
2 tablespoons tomato puree
1 tablespoon crunchy peanut butter
2 teaspoons yeast extract
1 pint/550 ml vegetable stock

garnish

chopped parsley

Sauté the onion in the oil in a large saucepan for 5 minutes. Add the tomato puree, peanut butter, yeast extract and stock. Bring the mixture to the boil, cover and simmer for 5 minutes. Serve garnished with chopped parsley.

PREPARATION AND COOKING TIME 15 MINUTES

Soups

Gazpacho Soup

SERVES 4

A chilled tureen of smooth gazpacho-style soup makes a splendid start to a summer meal. The soup can be swiftly prepared in a liquidizer, but it does need to be made with well chilled ingredients straight out of the refrigerator

1 lb/450 g ripe tomatoes
½ small cucumber, roughly chopped
1 red pepper, seeded, cored and roughly chopped
2 spring onions, roughly chopped
2 cloves garlic, peeled
juice of ½ small lemon
1 oz/25 g breadcrumbs
3 tablespoons olive oil
8 fl oz/225 ml chilled water
8 black olives, pitted and roughly chopped
2 tablespoons freshly chopped parsley
1 tablespoon freshly chopped chervil
1 tablespoon freshly chopped tarragon
8 well-crushed coriander seeds
salt and black pepper

garnish
a few sprigs chervil

Cut the tomatoes across horizontally. Lightly squeeze the halves to expel the seeds and excess moisture, then roughly chop them and place in a liquidizer. Blend till barely smooth. Pour this prepared tomato puree into a mixing bowl and set aside. Place the cucumber, red pepper, spring onions, garlic, lemon juice, breadcrumbs, olive oil, water and olives in the liquidizer and blend until smooth. Add this to the tomato puree in the mixing bowl, stir in the freshly chopped herbs and the coriander, and season with pepper and salt. Pour into a serving bowl and set aside in the refrigerator to keep chilled until needed.

PREPARATION TIME 20 MINUTES

Soups

Noodles and Chinese Cabbage Soup

SERVES 4

4 oz/100 g dried egg noodles
1 tablespoon vegetable oil
3 cloves garlic, crushed
1½ pints/850 ml vegetable stock
6 oz/175 g Chinese cabbage *or* other Chinese greens, thinly sliced
soya sauce to taste
4 oz/100 g beansprouts

garnish

1 tablespoon chopped coriander leaves
2 oz/50 g coarsely crushed peanuts (cover the peanuts with
a cloth and roll them with a rolling pin)
½–1 fresh *or* dried red chilli, seeded and finely chopped
½–1 tablespoon white sugar

Cook the noodles in plenty of boiling water according to the instructions on the packet or until just tender (about 5 minutes). Drain them and rinse under cold water until cooled to room temperature. Set them aside. Heat the oil in a large saucepan and sauté the garlic golden. Add the stock and bring to the boil. Put the cabbage in the pan and simmer for 2 minutes. Add the soya sauce to taste. Stir in the beansprouts and noodles and simmer until the noodles are heated through. Pour the soup into a tureen and sprinkle over the top the coriander leaves, peanuts, chillies and sugar. Serve immediately.

PREPARATION AND COOKING TIME 20 MINUTES

Chinese Egg Drop Soup

SERVES 3–4

1 large egg
½ teaspoon water
1¼ pints/750 ml vegetable stock
pinch sugar
pinch salt
few drops sesame oil
1 large shallot, chopped

garnish

2 teaspoons finely chopped chives

Soups

Beat the egg with the water in a small bowl. Bring the stock to a simmer and stir in the sugar, salt and sesame oil. Continue to stir while pouring the egg into the simmering stock. As you stir the egg will coagulate and form thin threads. Stir in the shallot and remove the pan from the heat. Pour the soup into individual bowls. Garnish with chives and serve.

Variation with beancurd To give the soup more substance, before adding the egg drop into the simmering stock 6 oz/175 g beancurd cut into ½ in/1.25 cm cubes.

PREPARATION AND COOKING TIME 10–15 MINUTES

Spring Nettle Soup
SERVES 4–6

The nettle is a valuable vegetable and can be cooked in the same ways as spinach. Young springtime nettles are especially good and they make excellent soup

2 tablespoons vegetable oil
1 medium onion, chopped
1 small clove garlic, crushed
1 large potato, scrubbed and chopped small
1 lb/450 g young nettles, chopped
1¾ pints/1 litre water
1 teaspoon lemon juice
½ teaspoon ground nutmeg
sea salt to taste

Heat the oil in a pan and sauté the onion and garlic for 2 minutes. Add the potato, nettles, water and lemon juice. Bring to the boil, reduce the heat, cover and cook for 15–20 minutes (until the potatoes are softened). Liquidize the soup in a blender with the nutmeg and salt. Reheat and serve.

PREPARATION AND COOKING TIME 25 MINUTES
FREE TIME 15 MINUTES

Soups

Curried Leek and Potato Soup

SERVES 4

This soup is a good winter warmer

2 tablespoons vegetable oil
1 large onion, chopped
3 large leeks, cut in half, washed and sliced and cut into small pieces
12 oz/340 g potatoes, scrubbed and diced small
1 teaspoon dried thyme
½–1 teaspoon curry powder
1½ pints/850 ml water
1 clove garlic
soya sauce to taste

Heat the oil in a saucepan and sauté the onion and leeks for 3 minutes. Add the potatoes, thyme, curry powder (according to taste) and water. Stir well, bring to the boil, reduce the heat, cover and cook for 15–20 minutes (until the vegetables are soft). Liquidize the soup in a blender with the garlic and soya sauce to taste, and serve.

PREPARATION AND COOKING TIME 30 MINUTES
FREE TIME 15 MINUTES

Watercress and Potato Soup

SERVES 4

2 tablespoons vegetable oil
1 large onion, chopped
1 clove garlic, crushed
1 teaspoon dried marjoram
1 lb/450 g potatoes, scrubbed and chopped
1½ pints/850 ml water
1 bunch watercress, yellow leaves discarded
soya sauce to taste

Heat the oil in a pan and sauté the onion, garlic and marjoram for 2 minutes. Add the potatoes and water, bring to the boil, reduce the heat, cover and cook for 15–20 minutes (until the vegetables are soft). Liquidize the contents of the pan in a blender with the watercress and soya sauce added to taste. Return to the pan, reheat if necessary, and serve.

PREPARATION AND COOKING TIME 30 MINUTES
FREE TIME 15 MINUTES

Soups

Spinach and Ginger Soup

SERVES 4

This is a tasty soup that is quick to prepare. Chinese leaves or watercress may be substituted for the spinach

2 tablespoons vegetable oil
1 in/2 cm piece root ginger, finely chopped
1 oz/25 g raw peanuts, dry roasted and crushed or 1½ tablespoons crunchy peanut butter
1½ pints/850 ml water *or* vegetable stock, boiling
10 oz/275 g fresh spinach, finely chopped
1 teaspoon cornflour
½ teaspoon ground turmeric
1 tablespoon dark soya sauce
½ teaspoon dark brown sugar
salt *and* pepper to taste

Heat the oil in a saucepan, add the ginger and stir fry it gently for 2 minutes. Add the crushed peanuts and stir fry for 1 minute. Pour in the boiling water, add the spinach and set the pan to simmer, covered, for 5 minutes. Combine in a small bowl the cornflour, turmeric, soya sauce, sugar, salt and pepper to taste and 2 tablespoons of stock from the soup. Stir the mixture into a paste, then stir the paste into the soup. Leave the soup to simmer, covered, for a further 10 minutes. Adjust the seasoning and serve.

Variation with chillis To pep up the soup add 1–2 finely chopped chillis when you cook the ginger.

PREPARATION AND COOKING TIME 25 MINUTES
FREE TIME 10 MINUTES

Soups

Miso and Vegetable Soup

SERVES 4

2 tablespoons vegetable oil
4 oz/100 g white radish (daikon) *or* baby turnips, finely chopped into matchsticks
1 small onion, finely chopped
4 oz/100 g carrots, thinly sliced
2 oz/50 g mushrooms, sliced
2 oz/50 g miso
1½ pints/850 ml vegetable soup stock *or* water

garnish

a few sprigs parsley *or* 1 sheet nori seaweed

Heat the oil in a heavy pan and sauté the radish, onion and carrots until just softened. Stir in the mushrooms and sauté for a further 1–2 minutes. Cream the miso with a little stock and add the remaining stock to the pan. Bring to the boil and stir in the creamed miso. Return the soup to a low boil and simmer until the vegetables are cooked (about 15 minutes). Serve garnished with parsley sprigs or toasted nori. Toast the nori by holding the sheet over a low flame and moving it back and forth for several seconds.

PREPARATION AND COOKING TIME 30 MINUTES
FREE TIME 15 MINUTES

Cream of Almond Soup

SERVES 4

1½ pints/850 ml vegetable stock
2 tablespoons butter
1 small onion, finely diced
2 tablespoons white flour
4 oz/100 g ground almonds

8 fl oz/225 ml single cream
salt *and* black pepper to taste

garnish

10 whole almonds

Bring the stock to the boil. Meanwhile melt the butter in a heavy saucepan and sauté the onions until just softened. Stir in the flour and blend well. Slowly add the boiling stock to the flour and onion, stirring the mixture all the time. Now add the ground almonds, stir well, reduce the heat, cover and leave to simmer for 15–20 minutes. Remove from the heat, stir in the cream, season to taste with salt and black pepper and serve garnished with whole almonds.

PREPARATION AND COOKING TIME 30 MINUTES
FREE TIME 15 MINUTES

Soups

Carrot and Oatmeal Soup

SERVES 4

2 tablespoons vegetable oil
1 large onion, chopped
1 small clove garlic, crushed
1 teaspoon dried rosemary
1 lb/450 g carrots, scrubbed and chopped small
½ teaspoon curry powder
1½ pints/850 ml water
1 level tablespoon medium oatmeal
sea salt to taste

Heat the oil in a saucepan and sauté the onion, garlic and rosemary for 5 minutes. Add the carrots and curry powder, cover with the water, stir well and bring to the boil. Add the oatmeal and cook, covered, over a moderate heat, stirring occasionally until the carrots are soft (about 15 minutes). Liquidize the soup in a blender, add salt to taste and serve. For a thinner soup, add more boiling water to the blender.

PREPARATION AND COOKING TIME 30 MINUTES
FREE TIME 15 MINUTES

Mulligatawny Soup with Yoghurt

SERVES 4

3 tablespoons vegetable oil
2 medium onions, diced
1–2 teaspoons curry powder
1 clove garlic, crushed
1 lb/450 g courgettes, diced small
12 oz/350 g tomatoes, diced

1 large potato, peeled and diced small
16 fl oz/450 ml vegetable stock *or* water
salt *and* black pepper to taste
garnish
2 fl oz/50 ml natural low fat yoghurt
1 tablespoon chopped parsley

Melt the oil in a large saucepan and sauté the onions for 2 minutes. Add the curry powder, garlic, courgettes, tomatoes, potato and stock. Bring to the boil and gently cook, covered, for 15–20 minutes (until the vegetables are soft). Season to taste. Puree the soup in a blender and serve garnished with a swirl of yoghurt and a sprinkling of parsley.

Variation with rice or pasta For a very substantial soup, heat the pureed soup through with 4 oz/100 g cooked rice or pasta before serving.

PREPARATION AND COOKING TIME 30 MINUTES
FREE TIME 15 MINUTES

Soups

Mushroom and Coriander Soup

SERVES 4

This soup and the cabbage soup below are simple Thai peasant dishes. They are quick to make and tasty

1 tablespoon vegetable oil
2 cloves garlic, crushed
½ teaspoon ground coriander seeds
¼ teaspoon freshly ground black pepper
2 teaspoons soya sauce
1½ pints/850 ml vegetable stock
4–6 medium mushrooms, wiped and thinly sliced

garnish

2 spring onions, finely chopped
1 tablespoon finely chopped coriander leaves
½ fresh *or* dried red chilli, seeded and thinly sliced (optional)

Heat the oil in a large saucepan and stir in the garlic, coriander and black pepper. Fry, stirring, until the garlic just turns golden. Add the soya sauce and stock and bring to a low simmer. Simmer for 10 minutes, then add the mushrooms. Simmer for a further 5 minutes and then serve the soup garnished with chopped spring onion, coriander leaves and, if you like hot food, chilli rings as well.

Variation with Chinese dried mushrooms Replace the fresh mushrooms with 4–6 Chinese dried mushrooms soaked in very hot water for 20 minutes, drained, their stems removed and discarded and the caps sliced.

PREPARATION AND COOKING TIME 30 MINUTES
FREE TIME 15 MINUTES

Chinese Greens and Coriander Soup

SERVES 4–6

Follow the mushroom recipe but replace the mushrooms with 8 oz/225 g cabbage or Chinese cabbage, thinly sliced. After adding the cabbage simmer for 6–7 minutes or until the cabbage is tender.

PREPARATION AND COOKING TIME 30 MINUTES
FREE TIME 15 MINUTES

Soups

The dip recipes given here form versatile additions to the vegetarian cook's repertoire. They are very quick to prepare with a blender, and when served with bread and a salad they make an excellent light meal. Dips are good starters and side dishes, and served with raw vegetables and bread for dipping they also make convenient buffet foods. For this chapter I have chosen nine substantial dips that are both very tasty and nutritious. Make a larger quantity than you need and keep the remainder in the refrigerator for later use – it saves getting the blender dirty twice. The spreads are very handy for preparing a quick, healthy snack or for making up sandwiches for a lunch box.

Incidentally, if you are in a hurry commercially available snack foods are very tempting, but be careful because they are often full of fat, sugar and salt. One other word of caution: many manufacturers, aware that healthy foods are now more popular, tag the words 'healthy' and 'wholesome' onto the most awful concoctions!

Dips & Spreads

Hummus Bi Tahini

SERVES 4–6

Hummus is the favourite bread dip of the Middle East
and Greece. Its individual ingredients do not look very
special, but combined they are delicious. An electric
blender also makes this a quick dip to prepare, whereas
by hand it is a laborious task

1 lb/450 g canned chick peas,
drained and the liquid reserved
4 fl oz/100 ml olive oil
2–3 cloves garlic

4 fl oz/100 ml lemon juice
5 fl oz/150 ml tahini
1 teaspoon salt
pinch paprika

Put half the chick peas into the blender and add three-quarters of the oil
together with the garlic, lemon juice, tahini and salt. Blend at high speed
until the mixture is smooth. Add the remaining chick peas slowly, with the
blender running. If the mixture gets too thick to turn, add some of the
reserved liquid. Finally, taste the hummus and add more salt, lemon juice
or garlic if needed. Pour and scrape the hummus into a serving dish, dribble
the remaining oil over the top, decorate the centre with a pinch of paprika
and serve. Hummus keeps well in the refrigerator for 4–5 days.

PREPARATION TIME 15 MINUTES

Two Cheeses and Walnut Dip

SERVES 4

1 tablespoon olive oil
6 oz/175 g cottage cheese *or*
cream cheese
1 tablespoon Parmesan cheese

salt *and* freshly ground black pepper
2 tablespoons finely chopped onion
1 tablespoon chopped parsley
1 oz/25 g chopped walnuts

Put the oil, cottage cheese, Parmesan cheese and salt and black pepper to
taste into a blender. Blend until smooth. If the dip is too thick add a little
milk and blend again. Add the onion, parsley and walnuts and pulse the
blender briefly to mix them in but not to crush them – the dip should be
speckled with bits of walnut, onion and parsley. Serve.

Variation with other cheeses and nuts The Parmesan cheese can be
replaced by 2 tablespoons grated mature Cheddar cheese. Try replacing the
walnuts with toasted almonds or cashews.

PREPARATION TIME 10 MINUTES

Dips & Spreads

Versatile additions to the vegetarian cook's repertoire, the dips shown here are
(*clockwise from the back*) Avocado and Lemon Dip; Two Cheeses and Walnut Dip; and
Red Bean, Lemon and Olive Oil Dip

Spreads can be whipped up in minutes to prepare a healthy snack with a green salad or to be used as sandwich fillings. *Above right*: Egg, Cheese and Nut Spread; and (*left*) Date, Cashew and Lemon Spread

Tahini and Lemon Dip

SERVES 4

This is a straightforward, quite thin tahini dip which is
also good, hot, as a sauce with grains or vegetables

4 fl oz/100 ml tahini
1 clove garlic, crushed
2 fl oz/50 ml water
juice of 1 lemon
1½ tablespoons vegetable oil (olive is best)
salt to taste

garnish

chopped parsley
pinch cayenne

Blend or thoroughly mix together the tahini, garlic, water, lemon juice and
oil. Put in more water if the dip is too thick. Add salt to taste. Serve
garnished with parsley and a sprinkling of cayenne.

PREPARATION TIME 5 MINUTES

Horseradish and Yoghurt Dip

SERVES 4

4 fl oz/100 ml chilled natural yoghurt
1–2 fl oz/25–50 ml horseradish cream
salt *and* pepper

Mix the yoghurt in a bowl with horseradish to taste. Season with salt and
pepper.

PREPARATION TIME 5 MINUTES

Horseradish and Peanut Dip

SERVES 4

3 oz/75 g crunchy peanut butter
2 tablespoons prepared horseradish cream
4 fl oz/100 ml single cream
2 teaspoons fresh lemon juice
salt to taste

Put all the ingredients into a blender and beat to a smooth cream.

PREPARATION TIME 5 MINUTES

Dips & Spreads

33

Green Chilli and Yoghurt Dip

SERVES 4

6 fl oz/175 ml plain chilled yoghurt
2 tablespoons prepared mayonnaise
10 black olives, stoned
salt to taste
4 oz/100 g tin mild *or* hot green chillies, drained

garnish
paprika

Put the yoghurt, mayonnaise, olives and salt to taste into a blender and mix to a smooth paste. Add the chillies and pulse the machine on and off until they are finely chopped but not completely blended in. Serve with a little paprika sprinkled over the top.

Red Bean, Lemon and Olive Oil Dip

SERVES 4–6

6 tablespoons olive oil
2 large onions, finely chopped
1 lb/450 g canned red beans, drained
5 tablespoons lemon juice
1 teaspoon honey
salt to taste

garnish

2 tablespoons olive oil
2 tablespoons lemon juice
3 tablespoons chopped parsley
1 teaspoon paprika

Heat the oil in a pan and sauté the onions until soft (about 5 minutes). Put the onions and oil in a blender with the beans, lemon juice, honey and salt. Liquidize until smooth. Transfer the dip to a serving bowl. Mix the garnish ingredients together and trickle the mixture over the dip. Serve.

Avocado and Lemon Dip

SERVES 4–6

2 medium size ripe avocados
juice *and* grated rind of 1 lemon
2 cloves garlic, crushed

salt *and* black pepper to taste
up to ¼ pint/150 ml vegetable oil
(olive is best)

Put the avocado flesh, lemon rind, lemon juice and garlic into a blender and make a smooth paste. Leaving the paste in the blender, add salt and black pepper to taste. Now put the blender on the slowest speed and slowly add the oil. Stop when the mixture no longer absorbs the oil easily or when the taste is to your liking.

PREPARATION TIMES 10 MINUTES

Dips & Spreads

Egg, Cheese and Nut Spread

SERVES 4

4 oz/100 g finely chopped *or* ground nuts

2 eggs, hardboiled, shelled and chopped

4 oz/100 g cheese, finely grated

juice of 2 lemons

salt *and* black pepper to taste

Combine all the ingredients and beat them to a smooth paste.

PREPARATION TIME 15 MINUTES

Date, Cashew and Lemon Spread

MAKES 14 OZ/400 G

7 oz/200 g ground cashew nuts *or* other ground nuts

5 oz/150 g dates, finely chopped

6–7 tablespoons lemon juice

Combine the ingredients and mix well together. Store any unused spread in a glass jar in a cool place.

PREPARATION TIME 10 MINUTES

Herb Butter Spread and French Bread

SERVES 4–6

3 teaspoons dried parsley
1 teaspoon dried marjoram
3 cloves garlic, crushed
4 oz/100 g soft vegetable margarine
1 large French stick

Preheat the oven to 350°F (180°C, gas mark 4). Mash the herbs and garlic into the margarine. Spread the mixture on a French loaf sliced down the middle. Put the two halves of the bread together, wrap the bread in foil, and bake for 15–20 minutes.

PREPARATION TIME 20 MINUTES

Avocado and Honey Spread

SERVES 2

1 ripe avocado and honey to taste

Scoop out the avocado flesh and mash it with the honey.

PREPARATION TIME 5 MINUTES

Dips & Spreads

Cheese Spread

SERVES 4

4 oz/100 g cottage cheese
2 oz/50 g Cheddar cheese, finely grated
1 stalk celery, finely chopped

1 tablespoon mayonnaise
pinch cayenne
salt *and* pepper to taste

Combine all the ingredients and mix well.

Variation with peppers and onions Replace (or add to) the celery with finely diced green or red pepper, onion or spring onions.

Variation with apple After putting the cheese spread on your bread, top it with slices of eating apple.

PREPARATION TIME 10 MINUTES

Tahini and Cumin Spread

SERVES 4

6 tablespoons tahini
1 clove garlic, crushed
2 teaspoons lemon juice

½ teaspoon ground cumin
1 tablespoon finely chopped parsley
(optional)

Combine the ingredients and mix well.

PREPARATION TIME 5 MINUTES

Miso-Tahini Spread

SERVES 2

2 tablespoons tahini
1 tablespoon miso
2 teaspoons lemon juice

Combine the ingredients and spread on wholemeal bread.

PREPARATION TIME 5 MINUTES

Peanut Butter Spreads

Combined with yeast extract (e.g. Marmite), miso or mashed banana, peanut butter makes delicious sandwiches. Spread slices of wholemeal bread with one of these combinations.

PREPARATION TIME 5 MINUTES

Dips & Spreads

Salads make almost the perfect fast vegetarian food. They are colourful, delicious, economical and – perhaps most important of all – nutritious. Many studies have been published in recent years confirming the importance of raw foods in our diet. Unlike other foods, they lose none of their original nutrients, fibre and essential enzymes in the cooking process.

Many of the salads in this chapter will stand on their own as light meals; alternatively they make excellent accompaniments to dishes from other chapters. Every salad recipe given here is suitable for inclusion in a high fibre, low fat diet. For those who can enjoy slightly richer food dressing recipes are given at the end of the chapter. Be careful, however, to choose a dressing appropriate to the particular salad you are making. Too strong a dressing will overpower a delicately flavoured salad, and vice versa. The dressings range from the mild, low fat Tofu (Beancurd) Dressing to the rich and highly flavoured Strong Cheese Dressing. Some of the dressings go equally well with the cooked vegetable dishes in the next chapter.

Salads containing dairy products have been included in the Egg, Cheese and Yoghurt Dishes chapter

Salads & Dressings

Apple and Celery Salad with Curry Dressing

SERVES 4

8 oz/225 g eating apples, cored and chopped
4 oz/100 g celery, thinly sliced
2 tablespoons lemon juice
3 tablespoons vegetable oil
½–¾ teaspoon curry powder
3 tablespoons natural yoghurt
salt *and* black pepper to taste

Combine the apple and celery in a serving bowl. Stir together the lemon juice, oil, curry powder and yoghurt. Add salt and black pepper to taste, and pour the dressing over the apple and celery mixture.

Variation with carrots and courgettes Another good combination with this dressing is carrots and courgettes. Replace the apple and celery by 8 oz/225 g carrots, coarsely grated, and 8 oz/225 g young courgettes, finely sliced.

PREPARATION TIME 10 MINUTES

Healthy Waldorf Salad

SERVES 4

2 red dessert apples, quartered, cored and sliced
2 stalks celery, washed and thickly sliced
2 oz/50 g unsalted peanuts
2 oz/50g whole hazelnuts
2 oz/50 g sultanas
4 fl oz/100 ml low fat yoghurt
1 teaspoon lemon juice

garnish

1 tablespoon chopped parsley

In a large bowl combine the apples, celery, peanuts, hazelnuts and sultanas. Stir in the yoghurt mixed with the lemon juice. Sprinkle the parsley over the top and serve.

PREPARATION TIME 10 MINUTES

Salads & Dressings

Double Beetroot and Apple Salad

SERVES 4

Raw beetroot and cooked beetroot have very different
flavours and textures, and this salad cleverly makes use
of both

1 large cooked beetroot, grated
1 large raw beetroot, grated
1 large eating apple, cored and cut into thin matchsticks
juice of ½ lemon
1 teaspoon grated lemon rind
1½ tablespoons vegetable oil
salt *and* black pepper to taste

Reserve a little of both types of beetroot and mix the remainder with the
apple. Add the lemon juice, oil and salt and pepper to taste, and toss the
salad. Mix the lemon rind with the reserved beetroot and garnish the salad
with this mixture.

PREPARATION TIME 10 MINUTES

Fennel and Orange Salad

SERVES 4

Like chicory leaves, fennel goes particularly well with
oranges

1 large head fennel, finely chopped (including the green part)
1 large sweet orange, peeled and chopped
1 oz/25 g raisins
vinaigrette dressing to taste (*see* p.49)

Mix the fennel, orange and raisins together. Add the vinaigrette dressing,
toss well and serve.

PREPARATION TIME 10 MINUTES

Salads & Dressings

Beansprout, Beetroot and Apple Salad

SERVES 4

Beansprouts are a rich source of vitamins, particularly vitamin C. They are cheap and available all the year round. Most beans and grains can be sprouted, as long as they are not too old to germinate. The most commercially popular sprouts are those from mung beans; other favourites are chick peas, kidney beans, soya beans and lentils. Beansprouts may be used fresh in salads or sandwiches, cooked in soups, omelettes etc., or in quick fried dishes in the Chinese manner

4 oz/100 g beansprouts	juice of 1 lemon
1 medium beetroot, sliced	1 tablespoon honey
1 medium apple, sliced	1 tablespoon vegetable oil
2 oz/50 g chopped nuts	pinch salt

Layer the beansprouts, beetroot and apple slices in a salad bowl. Top with chopped nuts. Beat the lemon juice, honey, vegetable oil and salt together and pour this dressing over the salad. Serve immediately.

PREPARATION TIME 10 MINUTES

Tomatoes in Hot Green Tomato Sauce

SERVES 4

6 medium size ripe tomatoes
2 spring onions, complete with green leaves
1 medium green *or* partially green tomato
1 tablespoon fresh coarsely chopped parsley
1 tablespoon cottage cheese
1 clove garlic
¼ small fresh *or* dried red chilli (*or* ¼ teaspoon chilli sauce)
salt *and* black pepper to taste

Quarter the ripe tomatoes and set them aside. Wash and trim the spring onions, removing any damaged leaves. Chop them roughly and place them in a liquidizer. Quarter the green tomato and add that and the rest of the ingredients to the liquidizer. Pulse for a few seconds at high speed. Test and adjust seasonings. Pour this dressing over the reserved quartered tomatoes, mix well and serve.

PREPARATION TIME 10 MINUTES

Salads & Dressings

Minted Chicory Salad

SERVES 4

Chicory is a very useful salad vegetable so long as its
slight bitterness is carefully complemented by the other
ingredients

½ small head lettuce, shredded
½ medium Spanish onion, finely sliced
2 heads chicory, cut into ¾ in/2 cm slices
1 sweet orange, peeled, sliced and chopped
2 tablespoons chopped fresh mint
2 tablespoons vinaigrette dressing (*see* p.49)

Layer the lettuce in the bottom of a salad bowl. Combine the other
ingredients in a mixing bowl and toss them well together. Pile this salad on
top of the lettuce leaves and serve.

PREPARATION TIME 15 MINUTES

Moroccan Orange and Date Salad

SERVES 4

This salad is best slightly chilled. If possible use fruit
and vegetables straight from the refrigerator

½ small crisp lettuce, washed
4 large oranges, peeled, pith removed, and sliced
4 oz/100 g dates, stoned and chopped
1 oz/25 g almonds, chopped, blanched and lightly toasted
1 tablespoon orange flower water (optional)
juice of 1 lemon
1 teaspoon caster sugar
pinch salt

garnish

cinnamon

Separate the lettuce leaves and prepare a bed of them in a glass serving bowl.
Arrange the orange slices, dates and almonds on top. Combine the orange
flower water, lemon juice, sugar and salt, mix well and pour it over the
salad. Sprinkle with cinnamon and serve.

PREPARATION TIME 15 MINUTES

Salads & Dressings

Tomatoes with Basil and Walnut Oil

SERVES 4

1 lb/450 g tomatoes, cut lengthwise into 6
1 medium onion, finely sliced
6–8 basil leaves, lightly chopped
salt *and* pepper to taste
1 tablespoon olive oil
1 teaspoon wine vinegar
heart of 1 small cos lettuce
2 teaspoons walnut oil

garnish

a few black olives

Place the tomatoes, onion and basil in a mixing bowl. Season to taste with salt and pepper. Toss lightly together and pile in the centre of a large serving plate. Dribble the olive oil and vinegar over the salad. Casually ring the central salad with the separate heart leaves of lettuce. Dribble the walnut oil over the lettuce and garnish the whole salad with a scattering of black olives.

PREPARATION TIME 10 MINUTES

Parsnip and Date Salad

SERVES 4

I'm not sure if parsnips are ever grown in the same areas
as dates, but they certainly taste well together

3 large parsnips, grated
8 dates, boiling water poured over them, drained and then chopped
1 tablespoon chopped fresh mint *or* ½ teaspoon crushed dried mint
vinaigrette dressing (*see* p.49)

Mix the parsnips, dates and mint together. Pour vinaigrette over the top to suit your taste. Toss and serve.

PREPARATION TIME 10 MINUTES

Salads & Dressings

Middle Eastern Salad

SERVES 4

Salads of lettuce, cucumber, tomatoes and onions are popular everywhere in the Middle East. The quantity of each ingredient used and the way they are combined depends on personal choice and local tradition. Below is one suggested combination. To make the salad more substantial add cubes of feta cheese and olives

1 small lettuce, shredded by hand
1 cucumber, thinly sliced
2 tomatoes, quartered
1 bunch spring onions, chopped
1 medium size mild onion, diced
1 bunch parsley, finely chopped
2 tablespoons fresh chopped mint *or* 1 teaspoon dried mint
1 clove garlic
2 fl oz/50 ml olive oil *or* other vegetable oil
3 tablespoons lemon juice
salt *and* black pepper to taste

Wash and prepare all the vegetables, the parsley and the mint. Rub the inside of a large bowl with the garlic. Combine the oil, lemon juice, salt and black pepper and add the clove of garlic, crushed. Mix well. Put the vegetables into the bowl, mix well, toss with the dressing and serve.

PREPARATION TIME 15 MINUTES

Caribbean Salad

SERVES 4

4 in/10 cm piece cucumber, quartered lengthwise and chopped crosswise
2 medium, just ripe bananas, thinly sliced
2 medium green peppers, seeded and diced
2 sweet oranges, peeled, pith removed, separated into segments and cut into halves
5 oz/150 g natural yoghurt

garnish

1 tablespoon flaked almonds, lightly toasted

Combine the cucumber, banana, green peppers and oranges in a salad bowl. Stir in the yoghurt, sprinkle the almonds over the top and serve.

PREPARATION TIME 10 MINUTES

Salads & Dressings

New Potato Salad

SERVES 4

This is a simple salad, particularly successful with the
first of the new potatoes

12 oz/350 g new potatoes
2 tablespoons chopped fresh mint
5 fl oz/150 ml tofu (beancurd) dressing (*see* p.52) *or* mayonnaise (*see* p.50)

garnish

chopped chives *or* parsley

Cook the potatoes in plenty of salted water. Keep an eye on them and remove the pan from the heat as soon as they are tender (press one between your finger and thumb – it should 'give' a little when cooked). Drain the potatoes and rinse them under cold water until cool enough to touch. Dice them and mix them with the mint and dressing. Garnish with chives or parsley and serve.

PREPARATION TIME 15 MINUTES

Israeli Fruit Salad

SERVES 3–4

In this fruit salad avocados are combined with citrus fruits, nuts and cheese to make a refreshing and nutritious salad which can also be served with bread or rice as a complete light meal

1 medium size ripe avocado, peeled, stoned and chopped
1 orange, peeled and separated into segments
4 oz/100 g mild Cheddar cheese, cut into small cubes
juice of 1 lemon
2 teaspoons honey
1 tablespoon chopped walnuts
¼ teaspoon ground cardamom

garnish

½ small lettuce

Combine the avocado, orange, cheese, lemon, honey, walnuts and cardamom and mix well. Chill briefly and serve on a bed of lettuce leaves.

PREPARATION TIME 10 MINUTES
CHILLING TIME 15 MINUTES

Salads & Dressings

Indonesian Fruit Salad

SERVES 4

2 Granny Smith apples, peeled and cut into pieces
2 oranges, peeled and segmented
1 grapefruit, peeled and segmented
½ fresh pineapple, peeled and cubed *or* 1 small tin pineapple
½ cucumber, sliced
1 bunch radishes, washed, topped and tailed
1 fresh *or* dried red chilli, seeded and finely chopped
1 tablespoon dark soya sauce
4 oz/100 g dark brown sugar
2 tablespoons white vinegar *or* 2 tablespoons lemon juice

Combine all the fruits and vegetables in a large bowl. Mix together all the remaining ingredients by hand or in a blender, and then pour this dressing over the fruit salad. Mix well and serve. The dressing can also be served in individual bowls into which the salad is dipped before eating.

PREPARATION TIME 20 MINUTES

Fig and Walnut Salad

SERVES 4

This colourful, crunchy salad is both tasty and nutritious. If fresh figs are available they can be used instead of the dried variety

½ small white cabbage, finely grated
3 medium carrots, scrubbed and grated
1 small onion, finely chopped
1 small cooking apple, grated
tofu (beancurd) dressing (*see* p.52) *or* mayonnaise (*see* p.50)
4 oz/100 g dried figs, sliced
1 dessert apple, cored and thinly sliced
juice of 1 orange
3 oz/75 g walnut halves

Mix together the cabbage, carrots, onion and cooking apple. Stir in the dressing. Put the mixture in a serving bowl and arrange slices of figs and dessert apples over it, leaving a space in the middle. Pour orange juice over the top and, lastly, heap the nuts in the middle.

PREPARATION TIME 15 MINUTES

Salads & Dressings

Mangetout and Avocado Salad

SERVES 4–6

If the mangetout are very young and tender just top and
tail them and use them raw in the salad. If a little older,
boil them very briefly as directed in the recipe. Buy only
the flat pods – those pods in which the peas have been
allowed to develop will already be stringy and starchy

1 lb/450 g mangetout, topped and tailed, and stringed if necessary
2 small to medium avocados, peeled, stoned and chopped small
2 oz/50 g small fresh mushrooms, finely sliced
2 tablespoons olive oil
1 tablespoon lemon juice
salt *and* freshly ground black pepper

garnish

2 tablespoons finely chopped parsley

Either use raw mangetout or drop them into a pan of boiling water, boil for
2–3 minutes, drain, and rinse under cold water. Combine the mangetout,
avocados, mushrooms, olive oil, lemon juice, salt and black pepper and toss
them well together. Garnish with parsley and serve.

PREPARATION TIME 15 MINUTES

Three Greens Salad

SERVES 4

8 fl oz/225 ml water
salt to taste
1 small head cauliflower, cut up into florets
2 courgettes, sliced into rounds
6 oz/175 g French beans, left whole
vinaigrette dressing (*see* p.49)

Add the salt to the water and bring to the boil in a saucepan. Put the
cauliflower in the pan, cover and simmer for 3 minutes. Add the courgettes
and beans and simmer for a further 5 minutes. Do not overcook, as they are
best a little crunchy. Remove the pan from the heat, drain the vegetables
and briefly rinse them under the cold tap. Drain them again and transfer
them to a salad bowl. Toss in a little vinaigrette dressing and leave to cool to
room temperature before serving.

PREPARATION TIME 15 MINUTES
COOLING TIME 15 MINUTES

Salads & Dressings

Two Colour Cabbage and Tangerine Salad
SERVES 4–6

Colourful, tasty and with contrasting textures, this Japanese winter salad is given a Christmas look by the tangerines

4 oz/100 g white cabbage, finely shredded
4 oz/100 g red cabbage, finely shredded
2–3 tangerines, peeled and sliced
2 tablespoons olive oil *or* sesame oil
1 tablespoon lemon juice
½ teaspoon salt

garnish

6 radishes, trimmed and chopped

Combine the shredded cabbage and tangerine slices and mix well together. In a small bowl stir together the oil, lemon juice and salt and pour this dressing over the salad. Toss the salad gently and then garnish it with the chopped radishes. Serve at once, or cover and refrigerate until needed.

PREPARATION TIME 10 MINUTES

Chinese Cabbage and Pomegranate with Poppy Seed Dressing
SERVES 4

½ largish Chinese cabbage (about 16 oz/450 g, thinly sliced crosswise)
4 oz/100 g young spinach leaves, washed, drained and chopped (optional)
1 pomegranate
4 fl oz/100 ml sunflower oil *or* other vegetable oil (cold-pressed if possible)
2 tablespoons lemon juice
1 teaspoon poppy seeds
1 teaspoon cider vinegar
1 teaspoon honey

Combine the Chinese cabbage and spinach leaves (if used) in a bowl. Cut the pomegranate and break out the seeds into the bowl, avoiding adding any of the bitter yellow skin. Blend the dressing ingredients together until smooth and pour the dressing to taste over the ingredients in the bowl. Toss well, turn the salad into a serving bowl and serve.

PREPARATION TIME 15 MINUTES

Salads & Dressings

Celery and Banana Salad and Spicy Dressing

SERVES 4

½ head celery, washed and cut into ⅜ in/1 cm sections
3–4 firm bananas, peeled and cut into ⅜ in/1 cm rounds
2 tablespoons cumin seeds
1 teaspoon coriander seeds
1 teaspoon cardamom seeds
7 fl oz/200 ml natural yoghurt
salt *and* cayenne to taste

Place the celery and the banana into a mixing bowl. Lightly toast the cumin and coriander seeds in a heavy metal pan until they begin to hop. Empty the seeds into a mortar, add the cardamom and grind lightly. Remove the cardamom husks before adding the spices to the yoghurt in a small bowl. Season the yoghurt with the salt and cayenne and stir well. Add the spiced yoghurt to the celery and banana and fold gently together. Turn into a serving bowl and serve.

PREPARATION TIME 15 MINUTES

Ginger and Soya Sauce Dressing

MAKES ½ PINT/275 ML

Serve with lightly cooked vegetable salads, rice and bean salads and root vegetable salads. This is a low fat dressing

1 tablespoon peanut oil *or* sesame oil *or* other vegetable oil
1 tablespoon finely grated root ginger
4 fl oz/100 ml soya sauce
4 fl oz/100 ml water
1 tablespoon cider vinegar
1 clove garlic, crushed

Combine the ingredients, mix well together and leave to stand for 15–20 minutes before serving.

PREPARATION TIME 5 MINUTES
STANDING TIME 15–20 MINUTES

Salads & Dressings

Basic Vinaigrette Dressing

MAKES 6 FL OZ/175 ML

5 fl oz/150 ml vegetable oil
2 tablespoons wine vinegar *or* cider vinegar *or* lemon juice
salt *and* pepper to taste
1 teaspoon prepared mustard (optional)

Place all the ingredients in a bowl or liquidizer and beat or blend well. Adjust seasoning if necessary.

PREPARATION TIME 5 MINUTES

Green Vinaigrette Dressing

MAKES 5 FL OZ/150 ML

This dressing goes well with starch-rich vegetables such as courgettes, with sweet vegetables such as tomatoes or beetroot, or with pasta

5 fl oz/150 ml olive oil
2 tablespoons lemon juice
½ bunch parsley, larger stems removed
1 teaspoon prepared mustard
salt *and* pepper to taste

Place all the ingredients in a liquidizer goblet and blend first at medium speed and then at high speed until a smooth sauce is achieved. Test the seasoning and adjust if necessary.

PREPARATION TIME 5 MINUTES

Japanese Mustard Dressing

MAKES 4–5 TABLESPOONS/60–75 ML

Use as a change from vinaigrette dressing, or with individual lightly cooked vegetables

1 teaspoon prepared English mustard
2 tablespoons rice vinegar *or* cider vinegar
1 tablespoon soya sauce
1–2 teaspoons sugar

Combine the mustard, vinegar and soya sauce in a small mixing bowl, add sugar to taste and stir well to dissolve the sugar.

PREPARATION TIME 5 MINUTES

Salads & Dressings

Basic Mayonnaise

MAKES ABOUT ½ PINT/275 ML

1 large egg
1 teaspoon prepared mustard
a good pinch salt
9 fl oz/250 ml vegetable oil
lemon juice *or* wine vinegar (up to 2 tablespoons) to taste
additional salt *and* black pepper to taste
paprika *or* cayenne to taste

Break the egg into a bowl or liquidizer goblet, then add the mustard and salt. Beat or blend at medium speed until the mixture thickens slightly. Still beating, pour in the oil from a measuring jug, drop by drop initially and then, as it begins to thicken, in a slow but steady stream until all the oil is absorbed. Carefully beat or blend in the lemon juice and season to taste. Store in a cool place. Mayonnaise will keep for not much longer than a day.

PREPARATION TIME 5–10 MINUTES

Tahini Dressing

MAKES ¾ PINT/450 ML

This, the most popular Middle Eastern dressing, can be poured over almost any fresh or cooked vegetable or served as a dip with hot bread. It is very simple and quick to make. The sauce can be thinned down if necessary, with water or more yoghurt. Tahini paste, produced by finely grinding sesame seeds, is widely available in ethnic food stores and wholefood shops

5 fl oz/150 ml tahini
5 fl oz/150 ml natural yoghurt
4 fl oz/100 ml lemon juice
1–2 cloves garlic, crushed
3 tablespoons finely chopped parsley
½ teaspoon ground cumin *or* slightly less cayenne
salt to taste

Combine all the ingredients in a mixing bowl and beat together. Taste, and adjust seasoning. Unused dressing will keep for 2–3 days in the refrigerator.

PREPARATION TIME 10 MINUTES

Salads & Dressings

Strong Cheese Dressing

MAKES 5 FL OZ/150 ML

Use this on red cabbage and curly or Batavian endive

2 oz/50 g strong blue Stilton cheese, or (if you can afford it) Roquefort
4 fl oz/100 ml strong flavoured oil: olive or walnut
2 tablespoons wine vinegar or cider vinegar
salt to taste

Mix the dressing as in the recipe below.

Mild Cheese Dressing

MAKES 5 FL OZ/150 ML

Use this on lettuce, celery and chicory

2 oz/50 g crumbled blue Stilton or fine diced firm Camembert or a mixture of both
4 fl oz/100 ml single cream
1 tablespoon lemon juice
salt to taste

garnish

fresh chervil or chives or dill

Combine the ingredients in a mixing bowl and lightly beat them together
with a small wire whisk. Taste, and adjust seasoning. Garnish the dressed
salad with the fresh herbs.

Coconut Dressing

MAKES 8 FL OZ/225 ML

A South East Asian dressing which is good on both
cooked and uncooked vegetable salads

4 oz/100 g fresh coconut, grated or 4 oz/100 g desiccated coconut
moistened with 2 tablespoons hot water
½ small onion, finely diced
pinch chilli powder or 2–3 drops chilli pepper sauce
2 tablespoons lemon juice

Put all the ingredients into a blender, then briefly pulse the machine to
form a well-combined but not completely smooth mixture.

PREPARATION TIMES 5 MINUTES

Salads & Dressings

Peanut Dressing

MAKES 12 FL OZ/350 ML

1 tablespoon vegetable oil
1 clove garlic, crushed
1 small onion, diced
4 oz/100 g roasted unsalted peanuts *or* 4 oz/100 g peanut butter
1 teaspoon brown sugar
1 tablespoon lemon juice
8 fl oz/225 ml water
salt to taste

Lightly brown the garlic and onion in the oil. Transfer the garlic, onion and frying oil to a blender and add all the other ingredients. Beat until smooth. Transfer the dressing to a pan, bring to the boil and then simmer over a low heat, stirring, for 5 minutes. Use immediately or allow to cool.

Variation with chillies For a spicy, hot peanut sauce in the South East Asian style, add 1–2 seeded, chopped red chillies to the garlic and onion in the pan.

PREPARATION TIME 10 MINUTES

Tofu (Beancurd) Dressing

MAKES 8 FL OZ/225 ML

Fresh white beancurd has the remarkable ability to absorb a whole gamut of flavours. Liquidize it with a little liquid, add your flavouring – be it mustard, paprika, honey or whatever – and you have an instant low fat 'mayonnaise'. Tofu dressings have a very high protein value and are cheap to make. Here is a basic dressing

6 oz/175 g fresh beancurd, drained
1 tablespoon chopped onion
1 tablespoon olive oil *or* other vegetable oil
1 tablespoon water
1 teaspoon lemon juice
1 teaspoon honey
salt to taste

Place all the ingredients in an electric blender, and blend together at high speed. Taste, and adjust seasoning.

PREPARATION TIME 5 MINUTES

Salads & Dressings

*I*n a vegetarian diet vegetable dishes are served in their own right and not as accompaniments to main courses. In this way the intrinsic qualities of the vegetables may be appreciated undiluted by stronger flavoured meat or fish dishes.

Some of the recipes given here are for parcooked vegetables, others for cooked ones, and three or four are for stir fried dishes. Whatever the method of cooking used, it is important that the colour, texture and flavour of the vegetables are not lost through overcooking or drenching in too strong a sauce. In some of the recipes a particular sauce is recommended, and in others the choice is left to the reader. A collection of simple and quick but tasty sauces is given at the end of the chapter. Some of the sauces go equally well with the salads in the previous chapter.

Vegetables are an important source of vitamins, minerals, fibre and carbohydrate to the vegetarian. Served with a protein source such as a cheese sauce, a tofu dish or a grain or pulse side dish, they provide a nutritionally sound meal

Vegetable Dishes & Sauces

Cold Stuffed Tomatoes

SERVES 4

2 oz/50 g ground almonds
1 oz/25 g wholemeal breadcrumbs
1 small clove garlic, crushed
¼ teaspoon curry powder
salt to taste
4 large tomatoes, halved, pulp removed and reserved

garnish

chopped chives *or* chopped parsley
4 lettuce leaves
4 slivers lemon

Combine the ground almonds, breadcrumbs, garlic, curry powder and salt and mix well. Stir in the tomato pulp and fill the tomato halves with the mixture. Top each with chopped chives or parsley, and serve on a lettuce leaf decorated with a slice of lemon.

PREPARATION TIME 10 MINUTES

Moroccan Cooked Salad

SERVES 4

2 medium tomatoes, quartered
2 medium onions, coarsely diced
½ cucumber, sliced in half lengthwise, seeded and sliced
1 red *or* green pepper, seeded and chopped
4 tablespoons water
3 tablespoons olive oil
2 tablespoons lemon juice
2 cloves garlic, crushed
salt *and* black pepper to taste
2 tablespoons chopped fresh coriander leaves

Put the tomatoes, onion, cucumber, green pepper and water into a pan, simmer the mixture for 4–5 minutes and then remove from the heat. Set the pan aside. Beat together the oil, lemon juice, garlic, salt and black pepper. Strain any liquid from the pan and then pour the dressing over the pan contents. Add the chopped coriander and gently mix. Transfer the salad to a serving bowl and serve warm or at room temperature.

PREPARATION AND COOKING TIME 15 MINUTES

Vegetable Dishes & Sauces

Tomato Oatcakes

MAKES 4 OATCAKES

Serve with salad and cheese for a delicious lunch

5 fl oz/150 ml tomato sauce made with tinned tomatoes (*see* p.70), liquidized
2 oz/50 g porridge oats
1 teaspoon yeast extract
1 teaspoon paprika
3–4 tablespoons wholemeal flour
salt to taste
corn oil *or* other vegetable oil for shallow frying

Mix together the tomato sauce, oats, yeast extract and paprika. Add just enough flour to make the mixture bind together well. Form the mixture into 4 round oatcakes about ¼ in/6 mm thick and coat them in flour seasoned with salt to taste. Heat a little oil in a frying pan and fry the oatcakes on both sides until golden brown (about 2½ minutes each side).

PREPARATION (INCLUDING SAUCE)
AND COOKING TIME 20 MINUTES

Stir Fry Watercress

SERVES 3–4

2 tablespoons vegetable oil
2 oz/50 g canned bamboo shoots, drained and shredded
4 oz/100 g button mushrooms, washed and drained
2 bunches fresh green watercress, washed and drained
salt to taste
1 teaspoon sugar
1 in/2.5 cm piece root ginger, peeled and chopped
1 tablespoon brandy (optional)

Heat the oil in a frying pan or wok and add the bamboo shoots and mushrooms. Cook, stirring, over a high heat for about 1 minute. Add the watercress and stir again. Add the salt, sugar and ginger and cook for 1 minute, stirring all the while. Add the brandy, if used, and cook for a further 5 seconds. Spoon the vegetables onto a serving dish, leaving any liquid in the pan. Reduce this liquid over a high heat, then pour in the liquid that has accumulated in the serving dish. Reduce again briefly, and then pour this sauce over the vegetables.

PREPARATION AND COOKING TIME 15 MINUTES

Vegetable Dishes & Sauces

Courgettes in Olive Oil and Lemon Dressing

SERVES 4

The courgettes are lightly cooked, and while still hot an
oil and lemon dressing is poured on them and they are
served immediately. Broccoli can be served in the same
manner. In each case the aromatic oil gives off an
evocative scent of summer as it is poured over the warm
vegetables

2–3 tablespoons olive oil
juice of ½ lemon
½ teaspoon brown sugar
salt *and* black pepper to taste
1–1½ lb/450–700 g small courgettes

Combine the olive oil, lemon juice, sugar and seasoning to taste. Mix well
and set aside.

Cook the courgettes whole in a pan of rapidly boiling water for 8–10
minutes. Test for readiness by giving each a gentle squeeze: once a courgette gives a little, it is cooked. Drain the courgettes and cool them briefly
under cold water. This will enable you to handle the courgettes more easily,
and it also helps keep their skins bright green. Top and tail the courgettes
and cut them up into ½ in/1 cm rounds. Place them in a serving bowl. Pour
the dressing over them, mix well, test for seasoning and serve immediately.

PREPARATION AND COOKING TIME 15 MINUTES

Savoury Potato Cakes

SERVES 4

8 oz/225 g raw potato, grated
2 medium onions, grated
4 oz/100 g plain flour
2 teaspoons dried sage
salt to taste
oil for shallow frying

Combine all the ingredients in a bowl and mix well. Form the mixture into
8 small, hamburger-shaped potato cakes. Heat the oil in a frying pan and fry
the cakes for about 5 minutes, turning them once during this time. Serve
immediately.

PREPARATION AND COOKING TIME 15 MINUTES

Vegetable Dishes & Sauces

Indonesian Fruit Salad and Moroccan Orange and Date Salad combine fruit and vegetables
to give colour and a hint of the exotic

From the back: New Potato Salad; Beansprout, Beetroot and Apple Salad; and Basic Vinaigrette Dressing. Salads make the perfect fast vegetarian food, being simple, economical and nutritious

Two-Colour Cabbage and Tangerine Salad and Three Greens Salad provide contrasting textures
and more substantial ingredients, making them perfect salads for the winter

While Japanese Skewered Vegetables should be served piping hot from the grill, with boiled rice as a side dish, Moroccan Cooked Salad can be kept and even improves its flavour the day after preparation

Chilli Hot Stir Fried Vegetables

SERVES 4

This South East Asian recipe can be used for a single vegetable or a combination. If using more than one vegetable, add to the pan first the ones that take longest to cook

1 lb/450 g total weight washed and chopped vegetables. Select one or more from:
beansprouts; cabbage, shredded; carrots, sliced; celery, chopped; courgettes, sliced;
French *or* green beans, stringed and chopped; green *or* red peppers, seeded and cut into strips
2 tablespoons vegetable oil
1 clove garlic, crushed
1 small onion, finely sliced
1–2 dried chillies, seeded and chopped
2 bay leaves
1 teaspoon grated lemon rind *or* 1 stalk lemon grass, chopped
2 teaspoons dark soya sauce
salt to taste

Heat the oil in a wok or pan and add the garlic, onion, chilli, bay leaves and lemon rind. Stir fry the mixture until the onion is softened. Add the vegetables (the hardest first) and stir fry until they are lightly cooked but still crunchy. Add soya sauce and then, if necessary, salt to taste. Stir well and serve.

PREPARATION AND COOKING TIME 15–20 MINUTES

Hot Potato Salad

SERVES 4

1½ lb/700 g new potatoes
2 tablespoons finely chopped onion
3 tablespoons olive oil

1 tablespoon wine vinegar
salt *and* black pepper to taste
4 tablespoons chopped fresh chives

Cook the potatoes in their skins until tender but still firm. Drain, peel and cut them into thick slices. Pour the oil and vinegar over them and mix very lightly. Add plenty of salt and black pepper and stir in three-quarters of the chopped chives. Turn the salad into a serving dish and scatter the remaining chives over the top.

PREPARATION AND COOKING TIME 20 MINUTES
FREE TIME 10 MINUTES

Vegetable Dishes & Sauces

Raw Radishes and Cabbage
with Hot Chilli Sauce

SERVES 4

A Chinese-inspired dish

1 lb/450 g white cabbage, finely shredded
1 bunch radishes, topped, tailed and thinly sliced
salt
3 tablespoons sesame oil *or* other vegetable oil
½ fresh *or* dried chilli pepper, seeded and finely chopped
2 teaspoons freshly ground coriander seeds

garnish

1 tablespoon coarsely chopped coriander leaves

Combine the cabbage and radishes with salt to taste. Heat the oil in a small pan and stir in the chilli and ground coriander. Cook, stirring, for 2 minutes and then stir the spiced oil into the cabbage and radish mixture. Sprinkle with coriander leaves and serve.

PREPARATION TIME 15 MINUTES

Coleslaw in Hot Sour Cream Dressing

SERVES 4

An unusual way of serving coleslaw, but it is rather nice
on a cold winter's day served as a side salad to a main
dish, or with hot soup and bread as a light meal

12 oz/350 g white cabbage, finely shredded
4 oz/100 g red cabbage, finely shredded
1 medium eating apple, cored and cut into thin matchsticks
2 teaspoons lemon juice
2 tablespoons milk
2 medium egg yolks
1 teaspoon prepared English mustard
1 teaspoon honey
1 tablespoon vegetable oil
4 tablespoons wine vinegar
salt and black pepper to taste
2 tablespoons sour cream

Vegetable Dishes & Sauces

Combine the white and red cabbage in a serving bowl. Stir the lemon juice into the apple pieces and then add the apple to the cabbage. Combine the milk, egg yolks, mustard, honey, oil, vinegar and seasoning in a blender or mixing bowl and beat until smooth. Transfer the mixture to the top of a double boiler or to a small, heavy pan over a low heat. Stirring all the time, cook the mixture until it starts to thicken. Put a little of it into a bowl and stir in the sour cream. Pour this back into the double boiler or pan and heat, stirring, until it is very hot. Pour the dressing over the cabbage, mix well, grind some black pepper over the top and serve. The coleslaw can also be heated through in the dressing and served very hot.

PREPARATION AND COOKING TIME 20 MINUTES

Sweet and Sour Stir Fried Vegetables

SERVES 4

The stir fried vegetables are only lightly cooked and should retain some crunch. This dish is very tasty and needs only boiled rice to accompany it. It can also be served cold as a salad

3 tablespoons vegetable oil
2 cloves garlic, crushed
1 medium onion, finely chopped
1 medium carrot, finely sliced
2 medium red or green peppers, seeded and cut into strips
8 oz/225 g white cabbage, finely shredded
6 radishes, sliced
6 oz/175 g beansprouts, washed, drained
2 tablespoons wine vinegar
2 tablespoons clear honey
2 tablespoons Tamari or other soya sauce

Heat the oil in a wok, saucepan or frying pan and add the garlic, onion, carrot and pepper. Stir fry over a medium heat for 3–4 minutes. Add the cabbage and stir fry for another 3 minutes. Add the radishes and bean-sprouts and stir fry for 1 minute. In a bowl mix together the vinegar, honey and soya sauce. Pour the mixture into the vegetables, stir briefly and serve immediately.

Variation with ginger If you like ginger, fry 2 teaspoons chopped fresh ginger with the garlic and onion.

PREPARATION AND COOKING TIME 20 MINUTES

Vegetable Dishes & Sauces

Broccoli with Coconut Sauce

SERVES 4

A vegetable other than broccoli (e.g. French beans, carrots, peppers or aubergines) or mixed cooked vegetables may be substituted in this recipe as long as the coconut sauce is prepared in the same way. Serve on its own, or as a side dish to a curry or other spicy meals, or as an unusual starter

2 tablespoons sesame oil *or* other vegetable oil
1 medium onion, chopped
2 cloves garlic, crushed
5 oz/150 g desiccated coconut
juice of 1 lemon
pinch cayenne
water *or* milk *or* coconut milk
1½ lb/700 g broccoli

Bring to the boil a medium sized pan of salted water. While it is heating, pour the oil into a frying pan and when hot add the onion and garlic. Stir fry until the onion is softened. Add the coconut and continue stir frying until the coconut is lightly browned. Transfer the contents of the pan to a blender, add the lemon juice, cayenne and salt to taste. Switch the machine on and add enough water or milk to form a smooth sauce that will easily run off a spoon. Pour the sauce into a small pan and heat through. Cut the stem ends off the broccoli and divide it into florets. Cook in the boiling salted water for 6–8 minutes and drain. Pour the hot sauce over the broccoli and serve.

PREPARATION AND COOKING TIME 20 MINUTES

Paprika Potatoes

SERVES 4

1¼ lb/600 g small potatoes, washed
½ medium onion, diced small
1 large red pepper, seeded and diced small
3 fl oz/75 ml mayonnaise (*see* p.50)
3 fl oz/75 ml natural yoghurt *or* sour cream
2 teaspoons paprika
pinch caraway seeds
salt to taste

garnish

chopped parsley

Vegetable Dishes & Sauces

Boil the potatoes in their skins until just tender but still firm. Cut the potatoes into bite sized pieces and turn them into a large mixing bowl. Add the diced onion and all but 1 tablespoon of the diced red pepper. Now add all the remaining ingredients except the parsley and stir well. Taste, adjust the seasoning and turn into a serving dish. Garnish with the reserved diced red pepper and the parsley.

PREPARATION AND COOKING TIME 20 MINUTES
FREE TIME 10 MINUTES

Vegetable Salad with Hot Sauce

SERVES 4 OR MORE

For this South East Asian salad suitably cut fresh vegetables are dipped into a hot sauce and then eaten in the manner of a French crudité. Select a number of vegetables from those suggested below, remembering to vary textures, colours and flavours. Arrange them on a large serving dish around a bowl of the hot sauce

celery, cut into sticks
cucumber, sliced
watercress, in sprigs
red radishes, whole
Chinese cabbage, coarsely chopped into strips
carrots, cut into sticks
green peppers, seeded and cut into strips
young green beans, left whole
chicory leaves
green apples, sliced and sprinkled with lemon juice
aubergines, browned in a little oil
courgette slices, browned in a little oil
2 tablespoons soya sauce
1 tablespoon finely chopped onion
3 cloves garlic
juice of 2 lemons
1 tablespoon sugar
chilli sauce to taste

Prepare all the vegetables and return them to the refrigerator while you prepare the sauce. Put all the remaining ingredients into a blender and blend to a smooth sauce. Pour the sauce into a serving bowl and serve as described above.

PREPARATION TIME 20 MINUTES

Vegetable Dishes & Sauces

Cos Lettuce in Cream Sauce

SERVES 3

1 good head cos lettuce	½ oz/15 g cornflour
4 fl oz/100 ml milk	2 oz/50 g peanut oil
salt to taste	½ teaspoon sugar
4 fl oz/100 ml vegetable stock	1 tablespoon butter

Cut out and discard the lettuce core. Separate the leaves. Leave the small ones whole and chop the larger ones into 4 in/8 cm lengths. Rinse and drain well, then pat dry. Combine the milk and vegetable stock in a bowl and set aside. Put the cornflour into a bowl and add about 3 tablespoons of the milk and stock mixture and set aside. In a wok or frying pan heat 3 tablespoons of the oil, and when it is hot turn off the heat. Add the lettuce and then turn the heat to high, cooking, turning and stirring the lettuce for about 1 minute. Add the sugar and salt to taste. Cook for about 3 minutes, then quickly transfer the lettuce to a serving dish with a slotted spoon. Wipe out the pan. Heat the remainder of the oil in the pan and add the milk and stock mixture and the cornflour mixture. Bring to the boil, stirring. When thickened, turn off the heat and stir in the butter. Add more salt if necessary. Spoon the sauce over the lettuce and serve immediately.

PREPARATION AND COOKING TIME 20 MINUTES

Middle Eastern Fried Potatoes

SERVES 4

1 ½ lb/700 g potatoes, peeled
3 tablespoons olive oil
1 small onion, finely chopped
2 cloves garlic, crushed
1 teaspoon ground cumin
4 oz/100 g black olives, stoned
salt *and* black pepper to taste

Boil the potatoes until almost tender but still firm. Drain them, and then cool under running cold water. Cut them into 1 in/2.5 cm cubes and pat them dry. Heat the oil in a frying pan and lightly sauté the onion and garlic. Add the potatoes, cumin and olives and stir fry over a gentle heat until the potatoes are tender and the olives very hot. Season to taste and serve.

PREPARATION AND COOKING TIME 25 MINUTES
FREE TIME 10 MINUTES

Vegetable Dishes & Sauces

Nut Kromeskies

SERVES 4

A kromeski is another name for a croquette. If you wish,
serve the kromeskies with tahini or tomato sauce (*see*
pp.68–70)

6 oz/175 g mixed chopped nuts	pinch ground nutmeg
1 medium onion, finely chopped	salt *and* pepper to taste
3 oz/75 g carrots, peeled and grated	2 eggs, beaten
4 oz/100 g fresh wholemeal breadcrumbs	wholemeal flour for coating
1 tablespoon finely chopped parsley	2 oz/50 g natural bran
1 teaspoon caraway seeds	vegetable oil for deep frying

Put the mixed chopped nuts on a baking sheet and lightly brown them
under a moderate grill. Mix them with the onion, carrots, breadcrumbs,
parsley, caraway seeds, nutmeg, salt and pepper. Mix in half the beaten egg
and stir well. Divide the mixture into 8 equal portions and shape each into a
round patty. Coat each kromeski in flour, followed by beaten egg and then
natural bran. Heat the oil and deep fry the nut kromeskies for 5–8 minutes
or until golden brown.

PREPARATION AND COOKING TIME 30 MINUTES

Tomato and Nut Balls

SERVES 4

These savoury nut balls are very quick to prepare. They
are good with a salad and pitta bread, and may also
be served with a cheese or tomato sauce (*see* pp.51 and
69–70)

1 medium onion, finely chopped	6 oz/170 g wholemeal breadcrumbs
1 small clove garlic, finely chopped	salt *and* freshly milled black pepper to taste
2 tablespoons vegetable oil	
8 oz/225 g tomatoes, chopped	*garnish*
4 oz/100 g nuts, ground or coarsely crushed	freshly chopped parsley

Sauté the onion and the garlic in the oil in a pan until softened. Add the
tomatoes and cook for another 5 minutes. Pour the mixture into a bowl and
add the nuts and breadcrumbs. Mix well. Season to taste with salt and black
pepper. Form the mixture into 2 in/5 cm diameter balls. Cover the tomato
and nut balls with masses of chopped parsley.

PREPARATION AND COOKING TIME 20 MINUTES

Vegetable Dishes & Sauces

Japanese Skewered Vegetables

MAKES 4 KEBABS

Skewered vegetables are cooked under a hot grill, and then served over rice or with bread. Vegetables other than those suggested may be used, but make sure they all cook at approximately the same rate – adjust cooking times by parboiling or by cutting the vegetables smaller or larger

12 button mushrooms, washed and drained
1 onion, quartered and each quarter halved
2 carrots, each cut into 4 pieces and parboiled in salted water for 5 minutes
2 green peppers, cored, seeded and cut into approximately 2 in/5 cm squares
2 tablespoons vegetable oil
2 tablespoons miso
2 tablespoons sugar
4 tablespoons soya sauce
¼ teaspoon cayenne

Preheat the grill at medium heat. Divide the vegetables in colourful patterns among 4 skewers, and brush with oil. Combine the miso, sugar, soya sauce and cayenne and mix well together. Grill the vegetables until lightly browned all over. Remove them from the grill and liberally brush with the miso mixture. Return to the grill and cook, turning so that each side is browned, for another 2–3 minutes. Serve immediately.

PREPARATION AND COOKING TIME 25 MINUTES

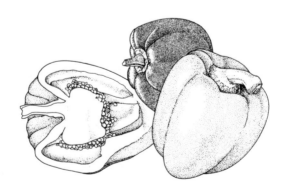

Vegetable Dishes & Sauces

The taste of summer is evoked in these vegetables, which can be served as separate dishes in their own right. *From the back*: Courgettes in Olive Oil and Lemon Dressing; Stir-fry Watercress; and Paprika Potatoes with Yoghurt Dressing

To spice up a bland savoury dish, try these delicious crunchy dishes: Sweet and Sour
Red Cabbage with Chestnuts; and Gado-gado with Peanut Dressing

Gado-gado

SERVES 4

Gado-gado is a popular Indonesian dish consisting of a mixture of raw and cooked vegetables served with a spicy peanut sauce either poured over them or in a side bowl. It is light, crunchy, tasty and good for you. The vegetables suggested here may be changed to suit availability or personal preference

1 tablespoon vegetable oil
1 clove garlic, crushed
½ medium onion, finely diced
½ red chilli, seeded and chopped *or* ¼ teaspoon hot pepper sauce
4 oz/100 g peanut butter
2 teaspoons brown sugar
2 teaspoons lemon juice
8 fl oz/225 g water
salt to taste
2 medium potatoes, peeled and chopped
2 medium carrots, peeled, cut in half and then thickly sliced lengthwise
4 oz/100 g French beans, topped, tailed, stringed and cut into 2 in/5 cm lengths
½ medium cucumber, sliced
4 oz/100 g beansprouts, washed, drained
½ crisp head lettuce, washed and chopped

garnish

1 hardboiled egg, sliced

Put a medium-sized pan of water on to boil. Meanwhile prepare the sauce. Heat the oil in a small pan and sauté the garlic, onion and chilli until softened. Put the contents of the pan into a blender and add the peanut butter, sugar, lemon juice and water. Process to a smooth sauce and then pour the sauce back into the pan. Bring the sauce to a gentle boil, stirring occasionally, add salt to taste and set on a low simmer. Put the potatoes in the pan of boiling water and cook until just tender. Meanwhile boil the carrots and French beans for 5 minutes only, in just enough salted water to cover them, and then drain. Arrange the cucumber, beansprouts, lettuce, cooked potatoes and parcooked French beans and carrots in a serving dish and garnish with slices of hardboiled egg. Serve with the hot peanut sauce either poured over the vegetables or separately in a bowl.

Variation with coconut milk For an authentic Indonesian-style peanut sauce substitute coconut milk (fresh or canned) for the water in the sauce.

PREPARATION AND COOKING TIME 30 MINUTES

Vegetable Dishes & Sauces

Nut and Vegetable Burgers

MAKES 4 BURGERS

Served as hamburgers in wholemeal rolls nut and vegetable burgers are delicious, nutritious and filling

2 carrots, grated
1 onion, finely chopped
2 sticks celery, finely chopped
4 oz/100 g cabbage, finely grated
1 clove garlic, crushed
2 oz/50 g roasted and ground nuts (e.g. almonds, peanuts, hazelnuts)
2 tablespoons wheatgerm
2 tablespoons wholemeal breadcrumbs, plus more for coating burgers
1 tablespoon plain flour
1 teaspoon dried mixed herbs
salt to taste
1 tablespoon milk
1 tablespoon tomato puree
2 fl oz/50 ml water
vegetable oil for frying

Mix together the carrots, onion, celery, cabbage, garlic, ground nuts, wheatgerm, breadcrumbs, flour and herbs. Whisk together the milk, toma-to puree and water and stir the mixture into the dry ingredients. Season with salt and form the mixture into 4 burger shapes. Coat them in breadcrumbs and shallow fry golden brown on both sides.

PREPARATION AND COOKING TIME 20 MINUTES

Gingered Courgettes

SERVES 4

1 lb/450 g courgettes cut into ½ in/1.25 cm slices
4 tablespoons vegetable oil
2 teaspoons finely grated root ginger
1 clove garlic, crushed
1 medium onion, finely sliced
pinch cayenne
3 fl oz/75 ml vegetable stock *or* water
1 teaspoon sugar

garnish

1 tablespoon finely chopped chives *or*
parsley *or* 1 sheet nori seaweed, toasted and crumbled

Vegetable Dishes & Sauces

Heat the oil in a heavy pan, add the courgettes and sauté for 3–4 minutes. Stir frequently. Remove the courgettes from the pan, then drain them and reserve any oil that collects. Put the courgettes to one side and return the reserved oil to the pan. Add the ginger, garlic, onion and cayenne and sauté over a high heat for 30 seconds. Reduce the heat, pour in the stock and sugar, and mix well. Add the courgettes and bring the mixture to the boil. Serve garnished with chives, parsley or toasted nori seaweed.

PREPARATION AND COOKING TIME 20 MINUTES

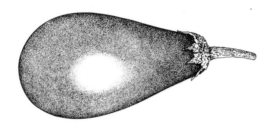

Aubergines and Tomatoes cooked with Soya Sauce

SERVES 4

Serve with boiled rice

2 tablespoons vegetable oil
1 medium onion, sliced
2 cloves garlic, crushed
4 small aubergines, thickly sliced, each slice cut in half to form a semi-circle
8 oz/225 g ripe tomatoes, peeled and chopped *or* tinned tomatoes, chopped
½ teaspoon chilli powder
2 tablespoons dark soya sauce
2 teaspoons dark brown sugar
salt *and* pepper to taste

Heat the oil in a saucepan over a moderate heat and sauté the onion and garlic until the onion is softened. Add the aubergines and sauté for 2–3 minutes. Add the remaining ingredients and mix well. Cover the pan and simmer for 10 minutes, stirring occasionally. Adjust the seasoning and serve.

PREPARATION AND COOKING TIME 25 MINUTES
FREE TIME 5 MINUTES

Vegetable Dishes & Sauces

Sweet and Sour Red Cabbage with Chestnuts
SERVES 4

1 medium onion, chopped
1 tablespoon vegetable oil
½ medium cooking apple, chopped
1 small red cabbage, thinly sliced
1 oz/25 g sultanas
2 teaspoons lemon juice
1 tablespoon brown sugar
2 teaspoons soya sauce
1 teaspoon cider vinegar
10 fl oz/275 ml water
1 teaspoon arrowroot made into a paste with 1 tablespoon water
4 oz/100 g tinned chestnuts

Sauté the onion in the oil in a pan for 5 minutes. Add the apple and cook for 1 minute. Add the red cabbage, sultanas, lemon juice, brown sugar, soya sauce and cider vinegar. Stir well and pour the water in. Bring to the boil, cover, reduce the heat and simmer for about 15 minutes. Stir in the chestnuts and thicken with the arrowroot. Cook, stir for another few minutes, and serve.

PREPARATION AND COOKING TIME 30 MINUTES
FREE TIME 15 MINUTES

Tahini Sauce
MAKES ½ PINT/275 ML

2 cloves garlic, crushed
1 teaspoon salt
4 fl oz/100 ml tahini
4 fl oz/100 ml water
juice of 2 lemons

Combine the garlic, salt and tahini in a blender and blend until smooth. Add the water and lemon juice and blend in. For a thicker or thinner sauce, use less or more water and lemon juice respectively.

Variation with yoghurt For a thicker sauce with a sharper flavour add 4 fl oz/ 100 ml natural yogurt to the tahini sauce.

PREPARATION TIME 5 MINUTES

Vegetable Dishes & Sauces

Béchamel Sauce

MAKES ABOUT ¾ PINT/450 ML

1 oz/25 g butter
2 tablespoons finely diced onion
1 oz/25 g wholemeal flour
½ pint/275 ml milk
1 bay leaf
pinch nutmeg
salt *and* freshly milled black pepper to taste

Melt the butter in a heavy saucepan over a low heat. Add the onion and sauté until soft and transparent. Stir in the flour to form a smooth paste and cook, stirring, for 2–3 minutes. Add the milk to the pan slowly, stirring constantly. Continue cooking and stirring until the sauce thickens. Add the bay leaf, nutmeg, salt and black pepper and simmer, covered, over a very low heat for 10 minutes. Stir occasionally.

Variation with cheese Stir 2 oz/50 g grated Cheddar or other suitable cheese into the cooked béchamel sauce until it has melted. For extra flavour also stir in 1 teaspoon prepared English mustard.

PREPARATION AND COOKING TIME 20 MINUTES
FREE TIME 10 MINUTES

Raw Tomato Sauce

MAKES 5 FL OZ/150 ML

Use good, fresh, ripe tomatoes for this sauce

18 oz/500 g ripe tomatoes, skinned and seeded *or* tinned tomatoes
1 tablespoon wine vinegar
2 tablespoons olive oil
1 tablespoon parsley, finely chopped
1 teaspoon dried oregano
salt *and* black pepper to taste

Place all the ingredients in a liquidizer and blend at low speed until a smooth sauce is obtained. Use cold or hot over delicate vegetables, either as it is or thinned with whipping cream.

Quick variation For a very quick sauce use tinned tomatoes in place of the fresh ones.

PREPARATION TIME 10 MINUTES

Vegetable Dishes & Sauces

Tomato Sauce

MAKES ABOUT 1½ PINTS/850 ML

2 oz/50 g butter *or* vegetable oil
1 medium onion, finely diced
2 lb/900 g tinned tomatoes, drained
4 cloves garlic, crushed
1 medium green pepper, seeded, cored and diced
2 teaspoons crushed oregano
2 tablespoons chopped fresh parsley
1 bay leaf
salt *and* pepper to taste

Melt the butter in a heavy saucepan and fry the onions over a low heat until soft. Chop the tomatoes into small pieces and add them to the onions with the garlic and green pepper. Stir well and simmer for 10 minutes. Add the herbs, and season to taste with salt and black pepper. Simmer for a further 10 minutes. Use immediately or allow to cool.

PREPARATION AND COOKING TIME 30 MINUTES
FREE TIME 20 MINUTES

Green Sauce

MAKES ½ PINT/275 ML

This is a good general-purpose sauce which you can use
on many young, tender vegetables, hot or cold

1 bunch good fresh watercress, well washed
1 tablespoon vegetable oil
5 fl oz/150 ml mayonnaise (*see* p.50)
4 fl oz/100 ml natural yoghurt
salt *and* pepper to taste

Trim the watercress of its roots and remove any discoloured leaves. Plunge the trimmed watercress into a pan of well-salted boiling water for little more than 10 seconds. This may seem trivial, but it greatly enhances the colour of the finished sauce. Drain the watercress and refresh it under cold running water until it is quite chilled. Squeeze the watercress free of any excess water, roughly chop it, place it in a liquidizer goblet with the oil and blend it to a smooth puree. Mix together the watercress puree, the mayonnaise and the yoghurt in a small bowl. Season to taste with salt and pepper.

PREPARATION TIME 15 MINUTES

Vegetable Dishes & Sauces

Sesame Seed and Soya Dressing

MAKES 5 FL OZ/150 ML

Method 1 gives a sour-sweet flavoured dressing that is best with crunchy, flavoursome vegetables. Method 2 gives a nuttier tasting, thicker dressing that is good with softer vegetables such as aubergines and courgettes. Tahini or Chinese sesame paste may be used in place of the crushed sesame seeds

Method 1

4 tablespoons sesame seeds
1 teaspoon sugar
2 teaspoons soya sauce
2 tablespoons water *or* stock
1 tablespoon rice vinegar *or* cider vinegar

Shake the sesame seeds in a dry pan over a moderate heat until they are toasted golden brown. Crush the seeds into a paste with a pestle and mortar. Combine the paste with the remaining ingredients and mix well to dissolve the sugar.

Method 2

4 tablespoons sesame seeds
4 tablespoons soya sauce

Toast and crush the sesame seeds as in Method 1. Combine the sesame paste with the soya sauce and mix well.

PREPARATION TIME 10 MINUTES

Speedy Chilli Sauce

MAKES 4 FL OZ/100 ML

Use this on lightly cooked green beans, mangetout, cauliflower or broccoli

2 tinned plum tomatoes, gently pressed free of juice
4 tablespoons vegetable oil
2 tablespoons hot pepper sauce
2 tablespoons soya sauce

Pour all the ingredients into a small, steep-sided mixing bowl and beat together with a fork or a small wire whisk.

PREPARATION TIME 5 MINUTES

Vegetable Dishes & Sauces

Coriander Cream Sauce

MAKES ½ PINT/275 ML

A soft, mellow sauce that's good with eggs (*see* p.107),
pasta and salads. It can be stored for up to 2 days in the
refrigerator, but is best made as required

1 bunch fresh coriander
5 oz/150 g cream
4 tablespoons sunflower oil *or* peanut oil
2 tablespoons lemon juice
1 tablespoon French mustard
salt *and* pepper to taste

Wash the coriander well and shake it dry. Cut away all but the finest stems.
Place the trimmed leaves in a blender container. Add the rest of the
ingredients and blend well together at medium speed until a smooth green
sauce is obtained. Test the seasoning.

Coconut Dressing

MAKES 8 FL OZ/225 ML

4 oz/100 g fresh coconut, grated *or* 4 oz/100 g desiccated coconut moistened with 2
tablespoons hot water
½ small onion, finely diced
pinch chilli powder *or* 2–3 drops hot pepper sauce
2 tablespoons lemon juice

Put all the ingredients into a liquidizer or food processor and briefly pulse
the machine to form a well combined but not completely smooth mixture.

Cream Dressing

MAKES 5 FL OZ/150 ML

This rich dressing can be stored for up to 4 days in the
refrigerator. Try it on fresh young vegetables such as
carrots, broad beans, broccoli or new potatoes

5 fl oz/150 ml chilled double cream
salt *and* cayenne pepper to taste
1–2 tablespoons wine vinegar

Season the cream to taste with salt and cayenne pepper. Whip it until it is
nice and thick. Gradually stir in vinegar to taste.

PREPARATION TIMES 5–10 MINUTES

Vegetable Dishes & Sauces

ereal grains, either whole or as flour products, are an excellent, well-balanced source of protein, vitamins, minerals and carbohydrates. Whole grain products such as brown rice take much longer to cook than the refined varieties, and for this reason I have had to compromise here between quick-cooking, whole grains such as oats, buckwheat and bulgar wheat (a parcooked wholewheat) and the refined grain products, white rice and white flour pasta. The main nutrients lost in the latter two products are fibre and some vitamins and minerals. In a balanced diet containing fresh fruit, vegetables and salads these deficiencies are more than compensated for in the other foods.

Rice is a particularly useful food for the cook in a hurry. While it is boiling, other preparation can be done. Some of the recipes given here are especially quick if leftover cooked rice is available, so cook more than you need and keep the rest in the refrigerator: store uncovered or in a container with a loose-fitting lid, otherwise it starts to go off after about a day. Long grain, pre-fluffed rice such as Uncle Ben brand is convenient and almost foolproof. Cooked pasta is also handy to have in the refrigerator for the fast preparation of fried noodle dishes. Again, make more than you need and store the extra. Stir in a little oil so that the noodles or spaghetti strands do not stick together. Bulgar wheat, used in a number of recipes in this chapter, is a wheat product made since ancient times in the Middle East. Since it cooks very quickly and has a delicious, slightly nutty flavour it is a most convenient product for the

Grains,
Including Rice,
Pasta & Bulgar Wheat

Boiled White Rice

SERVES 4

The cooking qualities of rice differ considerably depending on the source of the rice, its age and whether it is long or short grain, but the following general rules are useful:

1. 8 oz/225 g uncooked rice gives about 1½ lb/700 g cooked rice.
2. One volume uncooked rice gives 3 volumes cooked rice.
3. 2–3 oz/50–75 g uncooked rice per person is an average serving.
4. One volume uncooked rice requires 2 volumes water to cook it in.

The following recipe is a general one for packeted white rice. Rice bought loose needs a lot of washing and the process is quite time-consuming. Pre-fluffed rice is very quick-cooking and the quality is usually good – when cooking it, follow the instructions on the packet

1¼ pints/700 ml water
½ teaspoon salt
12 oz/350 g white rice

Bring the water to the boil in a heavy saucepan. Add the salt and then the rice. Return to the boil, reduce the heat, cover and simmer for 15–20 minutes or until the rice is puffed up, moist but not sloppy, and just tender (exact times will depend on the type of rice).

PREPARATION AND COOKING TIME 15–20 MINUTES

Simple Fried Rice

SERVES 4

This well-known Chinese dish is a really excellent way of using up any leftover rice or vegetables. It's best cooked very fast in a wok, but if you haven't got one use a large, heavy frying pan over a high heat

2 tablespoons vegetable oil
1 lb/450 g cooked rice
2 eggs, beaten
2–3 spring onions, chopped
soya sauce

Grains

Heat the oil in a heavy frying pan or wok over a high heat. Put the rice in the pan and stir fry for 2–3 minutes. Reduce the heat and pour in the eggs. Stir fry for 4–5 minutes. Transfer from the pan to a serving dish, sprinkle the spring onions and soya sauce over the top, and serve.

PREPARATION AND COOKING TIME 10 MINUTES

Rice Croquettes

SERVES 4

This is a good recipe for using up leftover cooked vegetables and/or cooked rice

1 lb/450 g short grain *or* long grain cooked rice
2 medium onions and 2 medium carrots, all finely diced *or* 1 lb/450 g mixed cooked vegetables
4 oz/100 g wholemeal flour
salt *and* black pepper to taste
2 eggs, beaten
wholemeal breadcrumbs *or* flour for coating
oil for shallow frying *or* deep frying

garnish

Parmesan cheese *or* Cheddar cheese, grated
parsley, chopped

Combine the rice with the vegetables, flour, seasoning and beaten eggs and mix well. Wet your hands in cold water to stop the mixture sticking to them, and form it into 8 croquettes. Roll the croquettes in breadcrumbs or flour. Now shallow fry them for about 5 minutes on both sides over a low heat or until nicely browned. Alternatively, deep fry them in hot oil for 3–4 minutes. Serve sprinkled with cheese and parsley.

PREPARATION AND COOKING TIME 15 MINUTES
ADD 20 MINUTES IF THE RICE NEEDS TO BE COOKED

Grains

Vegetable Donburi

SERVES 4

12 oz/350 g long grain white rice, washed and drained
2 tablespoons vegetable oil
2 small leeks *or* 2 spring onions, thinly sliced
1 medium carrot, grated
2 sticks celery, chopped
4 leaves spinach, chopped
4 oz/100 g mushrooms, sliced
2 tablespoons soya sauce
2 teaspoons sugar
salt to taste
2 eggs, beaten
black pepper to taste

Cook the rice by the basic method (*see* p.74). Meanwhile, heat the oil in a heavy pan and sauté the vegetables until just soft. Add the soya sauce, sugar and salt to taste. Pour over the mixture the beaten eggs, add a pinch of black pepper, stir and cook until the eggs are just set. Put the cooked, drained rice into a serving bowl, top with the egg and vegetable mixture, and serve.

PREPARATION AND COOKING TIME 20 MINUTES

Sesame Rice and Beansprouts

SERVES 4

12 oz/350 g long grain white rice, washed and drained
2 volumes of water to 1 volume of rice
1 tablespoon vegetable oil (sesame for preference)
1 clove garlic, finely chopped
½ medium onion, finely chopped
1½ tablespoons sesame paste *or* tahini
6 oz/175 g beansprouts
2 tablespoons soya sauce

Cook the rice by the basic method (*see* p.74). Meanwhile, heat the oil in a wok or frying pan and sauté the garlic and onion golden. Stir in the sesame paste and then the beansprouts. Stir fry until the beansprouts are very hot. Stir the mixture and the soya sauce into the hot, cooked, drained rice and serve.

PREPARATION AND COOKING TIME 20 MINUTES

Grains

Sultan's Pilau

SERVES 4

4 oz/100 g butter *or* margarine
1 lb/450 g long grain white rice, washed and drained
1¼ pints/700 ml water *or* stock
2 oz/50 g sultanas
pinch saffron *or* turmeric
½ teaspoon allspice
2 oz/50 g pistachio nuts *or* other nuts
salt *and* black pepper to taste

Melt the butter in a heavy saucepan. Add the rice and sauté, stirring, until each grain is coated with butter. Add the remaining ingredients except for 1 tablespoon of the nuts, and bring the mixture to the boil. Reduce the heat, cover the pan with a tight-fitting lid and simmer for 15 minutes. Remove the pan from the heat and allow to stand for 5 minutes. Meanwhile, lightly toast and then finely chop the reserved nuts. Tip the pilau onto a serving dish and garnish with the chopped, toasted nuts.

PREPARATION AND COOKING TIME 25 MINUTES
FREE TIME 15 MINUTES

Nut and Vegetable Rice Salad

SERVES 4–6

This salad is good on its own or stuffed into pitta bread

6 oz/175 g long grain white rice, washed and drained
4 oz/100 g red cabbage, finely chopped or grated
1 small green pepper, seeded, thinly sliced and chopped
1 small carrot, scrubbed and grated
1 oz/25 g sultanas
1 oz/25 g cashew nut pieces
5 fl oz/150 ml tahini dressing (*see* p.50)

Cook the rice by the basic method (*see* p.74). Meanwhile prepare the other ingredients and the dressing. Drain and rinse and cool the cooked rice under running water. Combine the rice with the red cabbage, green pepper, carrot, sultanas and cashew nuts. Pour the dressing over the salad and mix well.

PREPARATION AND COOKING TIME 25 MINUTES

Grains

Indonesian Rice Salad

SERVES 4

Despite its title the recipe is not authentically Indonesian, but it's a very good rice salad

8 oz/225 g long grain white rice, washed and drained
1 medium green pepper, cored, seeded and chopped
1 small onion, finely diced
4 oz/100 g beansprouts
4 oz/100 g tinned water chestnuts, sliced (optional)
1 oz/25 g sesame seeds, lightly dry roasted
2 oz/50 g cashew nuts, lightly dry roasted
2 tablespoons finely chopped parsley
4 fl oz/100 ml fresh orange juice
2 fl oz/50 ml olive oil *or* sunflower oil *or* other vegetable oil
3 tablespoons soya sauce
juice of 1 lemon
1 clove garlic, crushed
1 in/2.5 cm piece fresh root ginger, peeled and grated
salt *and* black pepper to taste

garnish

pineapple chunks
desiccated coconut, lightly dry roasted

Cook the rice by the basic method (*see* p.74). To make the dressing, combine the orange juice, oil, soya sauce, lemon juice, garlic, ginger and seasoning. When cooked, drain and rinse the rice under cold running water, and mix it well with the vegetables, seeds, nuts and parsley. Toss the salad in the dressing and garnish the top with pineapple chunks and coconut.

PREPARATION AND COOKING TIME 25 MINUTES

Hot Green Vegetable Rice

SERVES 4–6

2 tablespoons vegetable oil
2 leeks, sliced
1 in/2.5 cm root ginger, grated
1 clove garlic, sliced
1 green chilli, seeded and cut into strips
8 oz/225 g long grain white rice
8 oz/225 g spring greens, finely chopped
4 oz/100 g mangetout, sliced diagonally

Grains

Heat the oil in a frying pan or wok, add the leeks, ginger, garlic and green chilli, and fry quickly for 30 seconds. Add the rice, turning and stirring to coat each grain with the oil. Add sufficient boiling water just to cover the rice. Bring back to the boil, cover, and simmer for 5 minutes. Add the spring greens and the mangetout, bring back to the boil, and simmer for a further 7–9 minutes or until the rice is just tender. Drain, and serve immediately.

PREPARATION AND COOKING TIME 25 MINUTES

Spiced Rice

SERVES 4

The Indonesian name for this dish – nasi gemuk – means rice cooked in oil. In this recipe spices are fried in oil, raw rice is stirred in, and then coconut milk (traditionally used) or water is added and the mixture simmered until the rice is cooked

3 tablespoons vegetable oil
1 in/2.5 cm piece cinnamon
1 clove
2 cardamom pods, broken open
1 small onion, finely diced
2 cloves garlic, crushed
½ in/1 cm piece root ginger, finely chopped
½ teaspoon ground coriander
12 oz/350 g long grain white rice, washed and drained
salt to taste
1¼ pints/700 ml water or stock or coconut milk

Heat the oil in a heavy saucepan or wok and add the cinnamon, clove and cardamoms. Fry for 1–2 minutes. Add the onion, garlic, root ginger and coriander and stir fry for another 1–2 minutes. Stir the rice into the spice mixture, and add salt to taste. Carefully pour in the chosen liquid and bring the rice to the boil. Cover, reduce the heat, and simmer the rice for 15–20 minutes or until it is tender.

Variation with chillies If you like chilli hot dishes, add 1–2 finely chopped chillies along with the onion and garlic.

PREPARATION AND COOKING TIME 25 MINUTES
FREE TIME 10 MINUTES

Grains

Vegetable Paella

SERVES 4

Paella is a famous Spanish dish named after the large flat pan with two handles in which it is cooked. The pan doubles as a serving dish. A large frying pan and a serving dish do the job just as well, although a little of the drama of bringing the food straight from the stove to the table is lost

3 tablespoons vegetable oil
2 cloves garlic, crushed
2 medium onions, sliced
2 medium green peppers, cored, seeded and sliced
2 medium tomatoes, chopped
12 oz/375 g long grain brown rice
1½ pints/850 ml vegetable stock *or* water
salt *and* black pepper to taste
4 oz/100 g cucumber, peeled and diced
2 sticks celery, chopped
4 oz/100 g chopped nuts

garnish

2 oz/50 g olives (optional)
6 oz/175 g Cheddar cheese, grated

Heat the oil in a heavy frying pan and sauté the garlic and onions until they start to colour. Add the pepper and sauté for a further 2–3 minutes. Stir in the tomatoes and rice and cook over a low heat, stirring, for 5 minutes. Pour in the stock, season to taste with salt and black pepper, and boil rapidly for 5 minutes. Add the cucumber, celery and chopped nuts, reduce the heat to a simmer and cook until the rice is tender and all the liquid is absorbed. Add more water if the rice dries up before it is tender. Serve garnished with olives and cheese.

PREPARATION AND COOKING TIME 30 MINUTES
FREE TIME 10 MINUTES

Grains

Inspired by Japanese and Turkish recipes, these rice dishes are particularly useful for cooks in a hurry. *From the back*: Vegetable Donburi; and Sultan's Pilau

Grains, including pasta, bulgar wheat and wholewheat flour, are excellent sources of protein, vitamins, minerals and carbohydrates. *From the back*: Fried Noodles with Broccoli; Tabbouleh-filled Mushrooms; and Red Bean Tortillas

Plain Cooked Pasta

SERVES 4

Serve pasta with a sauce (*see* pp.68–72) and grated cheese, or on its own dressed with melted butter or olive oil and seasoned with freshly milled black pepper. The important rule when cooking pasta is to use a large pot and plenty of water. Cooking times vary depending on the type of pasta, and whether it is bought or home-made

4½ pints/2.5 litres boiling water
1½ tablespoons salt
1 lb/450 g pasta
a little oil *or* butter

Bring the water to a rolling boil. Add the salt, and about 2 tablespoons oil to prevent the pasta sticking to itself during cooking. Carefully feed the pasta into the pot and boil, uncovered, until it is soft on the outside but with a slight resistance at the centre, i.e. *al dente*. Shop-bought pasta will have cooking times on the packet. Fresh, home-made pasta requires 5–7 minutes. As soon as the pasta is cooked, drain it in a colander and serve.

PREPARATION AND COOKING TIME 15–20 MINUTES

Boiled Noodles

SERVES 4

Cooking times will depend on the type of noodle, and instructions will normally be given on the packet. Here is a general method

1 lb/450 g dried noodles
4½ pints/2.5 litres boiling water
1 tablespoon salt
2 tablespoons vegetable oil

Bring the water to a rolling boil, add the salt, oil and noodles, and stir gently. Cook the noodles, uncovered, in gently boiling water until they are *al dente* (about 5 minutes). Drain the noodles. If they are not to be used immediately, rinse them under cold running water, then drain them again and stir in a little oil to stop them sticking together. To reheat, pour boiling water over the noodles. To fry, see over the page.

PREPARATION AND COOKING TIME 15–20 MINUTES

Grains

Fried Noodles

SERVES 4

There are two ways of frying noodles: soft frying in a little oil, or deep frying in lots of oil. In each case the noodles are precooked, drained and cooled before frying

Soft fried noodles

5 tablespoons oil
1 lb/450 g cooked noodles

Heat the oil in a heavy frying pan. Add the noodles and sauté, stirring constantly, for 4–5 minutes.

Deep fried noodles

oil for deep frying
1 lb/450 g cooked noodles

Separate the cooked noodles into strands, fill a heavy pan or deep frying pan with 3–4 in/7–10 cm oil and heat to 350° F (180° C). Drop in the noodles, a handful at a time, and fry until medium brown. Remove with chopsticks and drain on absorbent paper.

PREPARATION AND COOKING TIME 10 MINUTES
TIME ASSUMES COOKED NOODLES AVAILABLE

Macaroni Salad

SERVES 4

This substantial salad is nutritious enough to serve as the major part of a cold main meal

8 oz/225 g macaroni
salt
6 tablespoons olive oil *or* sesame oil *or* sunflower oil
4 oz/100 g blanched almonds
4 oz/100 g mushrooms, sliced
½ small onion, diced
2 sticks celery, chopped
4 oz/100 g cheese, grated
juice of 1 lemon
pinch cayenne
1 oz/25 g sunflower seeds, lightly dry roasted

Grains

Bring a large pan of salted water to the boil and cook the pasta *al dente*. Meanwhile prepare the other ingredients. Drain the pasta immediately it is cooked and rinse under cold water. Put the cooled pasta in a serving bowl and stir into it 1 tablespoon oil. Fry the almonds in 1 tablespoon oil until just browned, add the mushrooms to the pan and fry, stirring, until softened. Remove the pan from the heat and stir the contents into the macaroni. Add the remaining oil and the other ingredients to the pasta, add salt to taste and mix well. Serve.

PREPARATION AND COOKING TIME 20 MINUTES

Summer Noodles

SERVES 4

The Japanese enjoy many foods cold that we in the West expect to eat hot. Chilled noodles –hiyashi somen – are a great favourite, particularly in the summer, when stallholders appear on the streets selling them in bowls. For a Western summer meal, chilled noodles make a welcome change from our usual salads and sandwiches. Soba (buckwheat) or wheatflour noodles may be used in this recipe

12 oz/350 g noodles
1½ pints/850 ml soup stock, chilled
3 tablespoons medium sherry *or* mirin
2 tablespoons soya sauce
pinch cayenne
2 teaspoons grated root ginger
3–4 tablespoons finely chopped parsley *or* watercress *or* spring onions *or* young spinach leaves

Cook the noodles *al dente* in plenty of boiling water. Meanwhile prepare the other ingredients. Drain the noodles and rinse under lots of cold running water until completely cooled. Divide the noodles among 4 bowls. Combine the stock, sherry, soya sauce and cayenne and divide among 4 more small bowls. Place ginger and parsley in central bowls and invite each person to garnish his or her own bowl. Each diner dips the noodles into the individual bowls of sauce.

PREPARATION AND COOKING TIME 20 MINUTES

Grains

Fried Noodles with Broccoli

SERVES 4

The method described in this recipe is a general one, and where I have given broccoli and celery as ingredients, vegetables such as carrots, beansprouts, Chinese cabbage, mushrooms and so on may be substituted

8 oz/225 g noodles
3 tablespoons oil
1 medium onion, diced
2 cloves garlic, crushed
1 in/2.5 cm piece root ginger, finely chopped
12 oz/350 g broccoli, chopped
3 sticks celery, chopped
dark soya sauce to taste
4 spring onions, chopped
salt *and* black pepper to taste

garnish

select from:
1–2 fresh *or* dried red chillies, finely chopped
fresh parsley, finely chopped
fried onion rings
thin strips of omelette

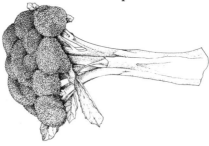

Drop the noodles into lots of boiling water and cook them *al dente*. Meanwhile start preparing the other ingredients. Drain the noodles and immediately toss them in 1 tablespoon oil, then set them aside. Heat the remaining oil in a large, heavy frying pan or wok and fry the onion, garlic and ginger until the onion is softened. Add the broccoli and celery and stir fry for 2–3 minutes. Stir in the cooked noodles, then stir fry them over a low heat for 2–3 minutes. Add the soya sauce and spring onions, season to taste with salt and pepper, and stir fry for another 1–2 minutes. Serve the fried noodles in individual bowls or in a tureen, and garnish.

PREPARATION AND COOKING TIME 25 MINUTES

Grains

Egg Noodles in Vegetable Stock

SERVES 4

A quick and filling dish, it is popular in Indonesia for a
speedy lunchtime meal

2 tablespoons oil
1 small onion, sliced
2 cloves garlic, crushed
2 pints/1.1 litres vegetable stock
1 in/2.5 cm piece root ginger, finely chopped
salt *and* black pepper to taste
4 oz/100 g cabbage leaves, shredded
1–2 fresh *or* dried red chillies, finely chopped (optional)
3 oz/75 g beansprouts, washed
4 spring onions, chopped
12 oz/350 g egg noodles
dark soya sauce to taste

garnish

select from:
chopped celery tops
fried onion flakes *or* rings
sliced hardboiled eggs
thin strips of omelette
tomato wedges

Heat the oil in a large pan and add the onion and garlic. Stir fry until the
onion is softened. Add the stock, ginger, and salt and black pepper to taste.
Bring the mixture to the boil, reduce the heat, cover, and simmer for 15
minutes. Add the cabbage leaves and chillies (if used), increase the heat and
bring the mixture to a gentle boil. Add the beansprouts, spring onions and
noodles. Loosen the strands of the noodles with a fork and stir in soya sauce
to taste. Adjust the seasoning and simmer the soup, covered, for 5–7
minutes or until the noodles are cooked. Transfer the contents of the pan to
a serving dish, and garnish before serving.

PREPARATION AND COOKING TIME 30 MINUTES

Grains

Muesli

SERVES 1

Muesli was formulated over seventy years ago by Dr Bircher-Benner. His recipe included a mixture of oats, raw fruits, nuts and milk. It was originally devised to provide a food that supplied good amounts of protein, vitamins, minerals and roughage without overloading the body with too much rich food and is now considered by most nutritionists to be an excellent food combination

2–3 level tablespoons rolled oats
1 eating apple, grated
1 teaspoon fresh lemon juice
2 level tablespoons natural low fat yoghurt
1 level tablespoon roasted chopped nuts
milk *or* cream to taste
honey *or* brown sugar to taste

Grate the apple just before it is needed and then combine it with the oats, lemon juice and yoghurt. Sprinkle the nuts over the top and add milk and honey to taste.

Variation with different fruit Use dried fruit, soaked overnight, or another fresh fruit in place of the apple.

Variation for delicate digestions Soak the oats overnight in milk. Muesli prepared this way is softer in texture and more digestible for some people.

PREPARATION TIME 5 MINUTES

High Energy Oat Cereal

8–10 SERVINGS

1 lb/450 g quick-cooking rolled oats
2 oz/50 g dried apricots, chopped
2 oz/50 g dates, chopped
4 oz/100 g sunflower seeds
2 oz/50 g raisins
4 oz/100 g mixed roasted nuts

Combine all the ingredients and serve portions of the mixture with milk, honey and chopped banana.

PREPARATION TIME 10 MINUTES

Grains

Oat and Herb Rissoles

SERVES 4

¾ pint/450 ml water
4 oz/100 g rolled oats
1 medium onion, finely chopped
1 teaspoon dried mixed herbs
1 teaspoon dried basil
1 tablespoon soya sauce

1 tablespoon tomato puree
salt *and* pepper to taste
2 eggs, beaten
wholemeal flour
wholemeal breadcrumbs for coating
vegetable oil for shallow frying

Bring the water to the boil and stir in the oats. Cook over a low heat for 15 minutes, stirring now and again. Add the onions, herbs, soya sauce and tomato puree. Season to taste with salt and black pepper. Add half the beaten egg and enough flour to make a stiff dough. Flour your hands and roll the mixture into small rissoles. Dip the rissoles into the remaining beaten egg and then roll them in the breadcrumbs. Now shallow fry until they are golden brown on both sides.

PREPARATION AND COOKING TIME 30 MINUTES
FREE TIME 15 MINUTES

Oatcakes

MAKES ABOUT 20 OATCAKES

8 oz/225 g medium oatmeal
1 oz/50 g wholemeal flour
1 teaspoon baking powder
2 oz/50 g soft vegetable margarine
boiling water to mix

Preheat the oven to 375°F (190°C/gas mark 5). Mix together the oatmeal, flour and baking powder. Rub in the margarine and add just enough boiling water to form a firm dough. Knead the dough well and roll it out to ⅛ in/3 mm thickness. Cut out the oatcakes with a plain 2½ in/6 cm cutter. Place them on a greased baking tray and bake for 10 minutes. Remove the trays from the oven, transfer the biscuits to a wire rack and cool a little before use. Store unused oatcakes in an airtight container.

PREPARATION AND COOKING TIME 25 MINUTES
FREE TIME 10 MINUTES

Grains

Plain Buckwheat (Kasha)

SERVES 3–4

8 oz/225 g buckwheat　　　½ teaspoon salt
¾ pint/450 ml boiling water　2 oz/50 g melted butter

Toast the buckwheat in a heavy, dry saucepan over a medium heat until it turns a deep colour and starts to smell nutty. Stir constantly to prevent it burning. Pour the boiling water over it, add the salt and cover. Reduce the heat and simmer for 15–20 minutes or until all the water has been absorbed and the buckwheat is tender.

PREPARATION AND COOKING TIME 20–25 MINUTES
FREE TIME 15 MINUTES

Buckwheat Noodles with Dipping Sauce

SERVES 4

This is a Japanese recipe in which buckwheat noodles – called soba in Japan – are cooked, garnished and served with a separate dipping sauce. Ordinary wheatflour noodles may be substituted if soba noodles are unavailable

12 oz/350 g soba noodles
4 tablespoons soya sauce
2 tablespoons mirin *or* sweet sherry
12 fl oz/350 ml vegetable soup stock
1 tablespoon miso
2 tablespoons toasted sesame seeds, crushed to a paste *or* 1 tablespoon tahini

garnish

2 tablespoons finely chopped spring onions *or* chives *or* young leeks

Cook the soba noodles in plenty of boiling water until *al dente*. Meanwhile, combine the soya sauce, mirin, stock, miso and sesame seed paste and bring the mixture to the boil. Drain the cooked soba and transfer it to one large plate or bowl. Divide the sauce among 4 bowls and garnish each with spring onions etc. Dip the noodles into the sauce before eating. Both noodles and sauce can also be served cold. The other way to serve the dish is to divide the noodles among 4 bowls, pour the sauce over the top and then add the garnish.

PREPARATION AND COOKING TIME 15 MINUTES

Grains

Millet Porridge

SERVES 2

This makes a delicious change from oat porridge

5 oz/125 g millet flakes
¾ pint/450 ml water
milk to taste
dates *or* raisins
maple syrup to taste (optional)

Mix the millet flakes with half the water in a saucepan. Add the rest of the water and cook until the mixture thickens (about 12–15 minutes). To serve, add milk with chopped dates or raisins, and add maple syrup for a special sweet treat.

Variation with rolled oats For traditional porridge substitute rolled oats for the millet flakes.

PREPARATION AND COOKING TIME 15 MINUTES

Buckwheat Pancakes

MAKES 8 SMALL PANCAKES

Once the batter is prepared and stored in the refrigerator, pancakes are easy to make for a quick sweet or savoury snack. Here is a recipe that uses buckwheat flour

3 oz/75 g wholemeal flour
1 oz/25 g buckwheat flour
1 tablespoon soya flour
salt to taste
8–10 fl oz/225–275 ml water
a little vegetable oil for frying

Combine the flours and salt in a bowl. Mix into them the cold water to form a medium-stiff batter. Beat well and then leave it aside for 15 minutes. Beat the batter again, and drop tablespoons of it into a small, oiled, hot frying pan. Turn when set, and brown the underside. Serve on their own with honey and lemon juice, or stuffed with leftover cooked grains, vegetables, savoury dishes etc.

PREPARATION AND COOKING TIME 25 MINUTES
FREE TIME 15 MINUTES

Grains

Buckwheat Croquettes

SERVES 4

8 oz/225 g uncooked buckwheat *or* 1 lb/450 g leftover cooked buckwheat
2 oz/50 g wholemeal flour
1 onion, finely diced
4 oz/100 g cooked vegetables, finely chopped, *or*
cooked beans *or* mushrooms, finely chopped
1 tablespoon soya sauce
water
oil for frying

Cook the buckwheat as in the previous recipe. Combine it with the flour, onion, vegetables and soya sauce. Mix in enough water (if needed) to form a firm mixture that will hold its shape. Form into balls about 2 in/5 cm in diameter or into burger shapes. Deep fry the balls in hot oil until golden brown, or shallow fry the burgers in a little oil in a heavy frying pan until both sides are brown.

PREPARATION AND COOKING TIME 30 MINUTES
FREE TIME 15 MINUTES

Buckwheat Spaghetti with Tomato Sauce and Sunflower Seeds

SERVES 4–6

Both buckwheat and wholewheat spaghetti have more
flavour and are more filling than regular spaghetti

1 lb/450 g buckwheat spaghetti *or* wholewheat spaghetti
5 fl oz/275 ml quick tomato sauce (*see* p.69)
6 oz/175 g sunflower seeds
2 tablespoons soya sauce

Preheat the oven to 450°F (230°C/gas mark 8). Cook the buckwheat spaghetti, in plenty of boiling salted water, according to the manufacturer's instructions or until it is *al dente* (about 15 minutes). While the spaghetti is cooking prepare and heat the tomato sauce in a saucepan. Also mix the sunflower seeds with the soya sauce, spread them on a lightly greased baking tray, and bake for about 10 minutes. Drain the spaghetti, and serve it hot covered with tomato sauce and topped with the soya roasted sunflower seeds.

PREPARATION AND COOKING TIME 25 MINUTES

Grains

Plain Bulgar Wheat

SERVES 3–4

8 oz/225 g coarse bulgar wheat
¾ pint/450 ml water
salt to taste

Dry roast the bulgar in a heavy saucepan over a medium heat for 2–3 minutes, stirring constantly. Remove from the heat, allow to cool for a couple of minutes and then add the water. Bring to the boil, reduce the heat, cover and simmer for 15 minutes or until all the water is absorbed. Add salt to taste towards the end of the cooking time.

PREPARATION AND COOKING TIME 20 MINUTES
FREE TIME 15 MINUTES

Bulgar Wheat Paella

SERVES 4–6

12 oz/350 g medium bulgar wheat
2 tablespoons vegetable oil
1 large onion, chopped
1 clove garlic, crushed
2 teaspoons fresh basil, chopped *or* 1 teaspoon dried basil
1 green pepper, seeded and chopped
1 large carrot, scrubbed and cut into rounds
14 oz/400 g tinned tomatoes, drained, chopped and the juice reserved
4 oz/100 g mushrooms, quartered
water to make tomato juice up to 1 pint/550 ml
soya sauce to taste

garnish

2 tablespoons chopped parsley

Roast the bulgar wheat in a dry pan over a low heat, stirring occasionally, until golden brown (about 5 minutes). Put it aside and heat the oil in another large pan. Sauté the onion, garlic and basil for 2 minutes over a low heat. Add the pepper, carrot, tomatoes and mushrooms. Stir well. Cover and cook for a further 5 minutes. Stir in the bulgar wheat, tomato juice and water. Bring to the boil, reduce the heat, cover, and simmer for 15 minutes. Add soya sauce to taste, and serve garnished with parsley.

PREPARATION AND COOKING TIME 30 MINUTES
FREE TIME 15 MINUTES

Grains

Tabbouleh

SERVES 4–6

Tabbouleh is a Middle Eastern salad made with burghul (bulgar) wheat, lots of fresh parsley and mint, and lemon juice. There is no specifically defined recipe. The recipe given here is therefore only a guide

8 oz/225 g fine bulgar wheat, soaked (see below) before preparing the other ingredients
8 oz/225 g onion *and/or* spring onions, finely chopped
2 bunches fresh parsley, chopped
4 tablespoons chopped fresh mint *or*
4 tablespoons crushed dried mint

3 medium tomatoes, finely chopped
4 fl oz/100 ml lemon juice
4 fl oz/100 ml olive oil
1 teaspoon allspice (optional)
salt *and* black pepper to taste

garnish

wedges of lemon

Cover the bulgar wheat with plenty of very hot water and leave for 25 minutes. Meanwhile prepare the other ingredients. Drain the bulgar wheat in a colander and squeeze out any excess water by gently pressing the wheat with your hand. Put the swollen wheat into a large serving bowl and gently stir in all the remaining ingredients except the lemon wedges. Taste, and adjust the seasoning. Garnish the salad with lemon wedges and serve.

PREPARATION TIME 30 MINUTES
FREE TIME 15 MINUTES

Tabbouleh Filled Mushrooms

SERVES 6

½ quantity of tabbouleh (previous recipe)
6 very large mushroom caps, stalks removed

garnish

mint *or* parsley sprigs

Set the bulgar wheat to soak and prepare the ingredients for making up the tabbouleh. Next, half fill a large saucepan with water and bring it to the boil. Put the mushrooms into the water and bring it back to the boil. Gently boil, covered, for 3 minutes and then drain off the water and set the mushrooms aside to cool. Make the tabbouleh salad, fill the caps with it, garnish with the herbs and serve.

PREPARATION AND COOKING TIME 30 MINUTES
FREE TIME 10 MINUTES

Grains

Tortillas

4 oz/100 g 100 per cent wholemeal flour
4 oz/100 g cornmeal
2 oz/50 g soft margarine
pinch salt
hot water

Preheat the oven to 350°F (180°C, gas mark 4). Combine the flour, corn-meal, margarine and salt and mix well to form a coarse meal. Add the hot water slowly to form a firm dough that does not stick to the sides of the bowl. Divide the dough into about 10 portions and roll them into balls. Flatten the balls on a floured board and roll them out into rounds about 6 in/15 cm in diameter. Heat an ungreased heavy frying pan over a moderate heat and cook 1–2 tortillas at a time. Turn them frequently until they are flecked with brown on both sides. Remove them to a moderate oven to keep warm, and cook the remaining tortillas. Cold tortillas may be reheated by the same method.

PREPARATION AND COOKING TIME 20 MINUTES

Cracked Wheat and Okra Pilau

SERVES 4

2 tablespoons vegetable oil
4–6 okra pods, washed well, stalk ends trimmed off
2 small courgettes, sliced into ½ in/1.25 cm rounds
1 red pepper, seeded and finely chopped
1 medium stalk celery, finely chopped
1 bay leaf
¾ pint/450 ml vegetable stock *or* water
6 oz/175 g cracked wheat
salt *and* black pepper to taste

Heat the oil in a heavy saucepan and add all the vegetables. Sauté them over a medium heat for 5 minutes. Add the bay leaf and stock and bring to the boil. Lower the heat and simmer for 5 minutes. Add the cracked wheat and salt and black pepper to taste and bring to the boil again. Reduce the heat to very low and simmer for 15 minutes. Look inside the pot after 10 minutes and leave uncovered if the wheat is too moist.

PREPARATION AND COOKING TIME 30 MINUTES
FREE TIME 15 MINUTES

Grains

Chapattis

MAKES 8

This Indian bread is normally eaten with curried foods
and other Indian-style savoury dishes

8 oz/225 g 100 per cent wholemeal flour
2 tablespoons vegetable oil
½ teaspoon salt
about 6 fl oz/175 ml water

Preheat the oven to 350°F (180°C/gas mark 4). Mix the flour, oil, salt and water in a bowl to form a fairly stiff dough that comes away from the side of the bowl. Knead the dough until the texture is smooth and elastic. Divide it into 8 portions and roll them into balls. Flatten the balls on a floured board and roll them out thinly into circles approximately 8 in/20 cm in diameter. Heat an ungreased heavy frying pan over a high heat. Place a chapatti in it, cook the chapatti for about 1 minute and then turn it over. Press the edges with a spatula – they should puff up slightly. Continue cooking until the underside is just mottled with brown spots. Remove the chapatti from the pan and store it in a moderate oven or wrap in a clean cloth to keep it warm while you cook the others.

PREPARATION AND COOKING TIME 20 MINUTES

Grains

*B*eans, peas and lentils are the seeds of the plant family known as legumes or pulses. They grow in a wide range of climates and provide a good source of protein and carbohydrate for vegetarians. Unfortunately for the cook in a hurry, nearly all dried beans and peas (the form in which they are normally sold) need lengthy soaking and cooking to make them digestible. I have therefore chosen recipes that use easily available tinned beans, e.g. red beans, chick peas and haricot beans. Fortunately, these beans are relatively successful when tinned and they are very useful foods in the armoury of the 30-Minute Vegetarian.

Two soya bean products have also been included in this chapter. They are tofu, also called beancurd, and tempe. Tofu, used in several recipes in other chapters, is now quite an easily available ingredient, tempe less so. Both products are convenient, versatile foods to use in fast vegetarian cookery, and are good sources of protein, carbohydrate and minerals. Tofu is particularly useful in making low fat dressings for salads and, fluffed up with a little honey in a blender, it even makes a tasty dressing for fruit salads. Add tofu also to soups, vegetables and salads to give them extra body

Pulses,
Including tofu & tempe

Falafel

Spiced chick pea balls, fried golden brown. Serve with
wedges of lemon, green salad, pitta bread and a bowl of
tahini sauce (*see* p.50)

1½ lb/700 g canned chick peas, drained
3 cloves garlic
2 teaspoons ground coriander
2 teaspoons ground cumin
2 tablespoons lemon juice
2 tablespoons chopped parsley
sea salt to taste
oil for shallow frying

Put a quarter of the chick peas into a blender with the garlic, coriander, cumin, lemon juice and parsley. Liquidize, and keep adding a few more chick peas and then blending until they are all in. You will need to add some water to get them to liquidize, but use as little as possible to get them through. Season the mixture with salt and transfer it to a bowl. Take dessertspoons of the mixture and shape it into round balls. Heat the oil in a frying pan and fry the falafel in batches for 2–3 minutes or until golden brown all over. Drain well and serve.

PREPARATION AND COOKING TIME 30 MINUTES

Haricot Bean and Sweet-Sour Beetroot Salad

SERVES 4

2 medium cooked beetroot, medium diced
1 tablespoon butter
2 teaspoons cider vinegar
2 teaspoons honey
8 oz/225 g canned haricot beans, drained
salt to taste
2 tablespoons sour cream *or* plain yoghurt

Put the beetroot in a pan with the butter and gently heat to melt the butter. Stir, and add the vinegar and honey. Continue heating to melt the honey, and coat the beetroot in the sauce. Pour this mixture over the beans, stir well, and add salt to taste. Serve dressed in sour cream or yoghurt.

PREPARATION AND COOKING TIME 15 MINUTES

Pulses

A filling and tasty winter salad, Haricot Bean and Sweet-Sour Beetroot Salad also makes an excellent light lunch with a crust of bread and a hunk of cheese

Buckwheat Omelette and Baked Tomatoes with Walnut and Cottage Cheese Filling served together make a delicious, wholesome and substantial meal

Red Bean Stuffed Tortillas

SERVES 4

Tortillas are thin pancakes made with a maize flour dough. They are served here with a kidney bean filling and covered with tomato sauce. Stuffed tortillas are known in Mexico as tacos

2 tablespoons vegetable oil
1 small onion, coarsely chopped
½ green pepper, seeded and coarsely chopped
1 small dried chilli, seeded and finely chopped
1 clove garlic, crushed
1 lb/450g canned red beans
6 fl oz/175 ml quick tomato sauce (*see* p.69)
1 teaspoon chilli powder
½ teaspoon ground cumin
salt *and* black pepper
8 cooked tortillas (shop-bought, or for preparation *see* p.93)

garnish

¼ head lettuce, shredded
4 tomatoes, coarsely chopped
4 oz (100 g) Cheddar cheese, grated

Preheat the oven to 350°F (180°C/gas mark 4). In a large pan heat the oil over a medium heat. Add the onion, peppers and dried chilli. Cook until tender. Add the garlic, beans, tomato sauce, chilli powder and cumin, and season with salt and pepper. Cover, and simmer gently over a low heat for 5 minutes. Place the tortillas on a baking sheet and bake for 5 minutes. Fill each tortilla shell with a portion of the bean mixture. Fold them up and place 2 to a plate. Top with lettuce, tomatoes and cheese. Serve immediately.

PREPARATION AND COOKING TIME 30 MINUTES
INCLUDING TOMATO SAUCE

Pulses

Four Colour Salad with Japanese White Dressing

SERVES 4

A Japanese-inspired tofu-dressed salad which combines different colours, shapes, tastes and textures in a delicious and healthy way. Serve as a starter or as an accompaniment to a main meal. It is particularly good with spiced and/or chilli hot dishes, when its cooling, sweetish flavour is much appreciated

4 oz/100 g white radish (daikon), peeled and cut into matchsticks
4 oz/100 g carrots, peeled and cut into thin rounds
4 oz/100 g green beans, topped, tailed and stringed if needed
2 oz/50 g dried apricots, washed and finely chopped
tofu dressing (*see* p.52)

Parboil the radish and carrots in lightly salted boiling water for just 2 minutes. Drain, and rinse immediately under cold water. Parboil the beans in the same way, but for 3 minutes. Combine the vegetables and dried apricots and stir the dressing into them. Serve the salad arranged in neat mounds on individual small plates.

PREPARATION AND COOKING TIME 15 MINUTES

Fried Tempe

SERVES 4

Fried tempe is very pleasant served as a snack or side dish, lightly sprinkled with salt

12 oz/350 g tempe, cut into sticks about 2 × ¼ × ½ in/5 × 1 × ½ cm
oil for deep frying
salt to taste

Heat about 1 in/2.5 cm of oil in a deep frying pan over a medium heat. Add half the tempe sticks and fry, stirring, until they turn golden brown (about 5 minutes). Remove them with a small sieve or slotted spoon and set them to drain on absorbent kitchen paper. Put in a warm place while you fry the remaining tempe. Combine the 2 batches of tempe, sprinkle with salt and serve.

PREPARATION AND COOKING TIME 15 MINUTES

Pulses

Fried Tempe in Hot Sauce
SERVES 4
Ingredients as for fried tempe recipe, plus:

1 medium onion, finely chopped
2 cloves garlic
2 fresh *or* dried red chillies, seeded
2 fl oz/50 ml water
2 teaspoons brown sugar
1 teaspoon salt

Fry the tempe sticks as described and keep the fried sticks hot in a warm oven. Put the onion, garlic, chillies and water into a blender or food processor and blend them to a paste. Remove all but 2 tablespoons of oil from the frying pan in which the tempe was fried. Add the paste and stir fry for 4–5 minutes. Stir in the sugar and salt and then the fried tempe. Mix well and serve immediately.

PREPARATION AND COOKING TIME 25 MINUTES

Seasoned and Fried Tempe
SERVES 4
12 oz/350 g tempe, cut into sticks about 2 × ¼ × ½ in/5 × 1 × ½ cm
2 cloves garlic, crushed
1 teaspoon salt
½ teaspoon freshly ground pepper
1 teaspoon ground coriander
4 fl oz/100 ml water *or* vegetable stock *or* wine
juice of 1 lemon
oil for deep frying

Mix together in a bowl all the ingredients, except the tempe and oil, and then add the tempe sticks. Stir them about in the bowl to coat each stick with the seasoning. Leave them to marinate for 5–10 minutes. Set a sieve over a bowl. Remove the sticks and leave them to drain for a few minutes in the sieve. Deep fry the seasoned tempe as described in the previous recipe. Serve with the collected marinade as a dipping sauce.

PREPARATION AND COOKING TIME 30 MINUTES

Pulses

Deep Fried Tofu and Dipping Sauce

SERVES 2

Roll 2 pieces of tofu about 3 in/6 cm square in cornflour, taking care not to break them. Then deep fry them over a moderate heat (325°F/170°C) for 4 minutes until light golden in colour. Lift the tofu out carefully, and drain. Eat hot with one of the following dipping sauces, made by merely combining the ingredients listed

Sauce 1

2 teaspoons sesame oil
¼ teaspoon hot pepper sauce
1 clove garlic, crushed
2 teaspoons grated root ginger
2 spring onions, finely chopped

Sauce 2

3 tablespoons dark soya sauce
1 tablespoon prepared mustard
1 teaspoon dark brown sugar
1 teaspoon rice vinegar *or* cider vinegar
1 teaspoon minced spring onion

Sauce 3

2 tablespoons sherry
3 tablespoons dark soya sauce
1 teaspoon sugar

PREPARATION AND COOKING TIME 15 MINUTES

Tofu Burgers

SERVES 4

Delicious, low fat burgers. Serve, if you wish, with a sauce (*see* pp.68–72)

4 tablespoons vegetable oil
½ medium onion, finely diced
1 small green pepper, seeded and finely diced
1 medium carrot, grated
12 oz/350 g tofu, drained
2 tablespoons wholemeal flour
1 egg, beaten
4 oz/100 g cheese, grated
salt to taste
wholemeal flour for dusting

Heat half the oil in a frying pan and add the onion, pepper and carrot. Stir fry until the onion is softened. Mash the tofu in a mixing bowl and add the fried vegetables, flour, egg, cheese and salt. Mix well and then, with wet hands, form the mixture into about 12 small burger shapes. Dust them with flour and fry them brown on both sides in the remaining oil.

PREPARATION AND COOKING TIME 25 MINUTES

Pulses

Vegetable and Tofu Salad

SERVES 4–6

2 tablespoons peanut oil *or* sesame oil *or* other vegetable oil
3 tablespoons soya sauce
3 tablespoons cider vinegar
1 tablespoon water
1 teaspoon clear honey
1 clove garlic, crushed
2 blocks tofu beancurd, cut into 1 in/2.5 cm cubes
2 stalks celery, finely chopped
2 oz/50 g mushrooms, washed and sliced
4 oz/100 g Chinese cabbage *or* drumhead cabbage, finely shredded

Combine the oil, soya sauce, vinegar, water, honey and garlic and mix well together. Put two-thirds of this mixture into a large, shallow bowl or container and add the tofu cubes. Leave them to marinate in it for 15 minutes in the refrigerator. Meanwhile prepare the other ingredients. Transfer the tofu and marinade to a serving bowl and gently stir in the celery, mushrooms and cabbage. Carefully toss the salad and serve.

PREPARATION AND CHILLING TIME 25 MINUTES

Fried Tofu

SERVES 4

Fried tofu is good both as a snack served on its own or
with a chilli sauce (*see* p.70), or with other dishes as part
of a larger meal

4 cakes fresh medium hard tofu about 4 oz/100 g each, cut into 1 in/2.5 cm cubes
oil for deep frying
2 tablespoons dark soya sauce

garnish

4 spring onions, finely chopped

Heat about 2 in/5 cm of the oil in a pan and deep fry the tofu cubes, a few at a time, until crisp and golden brown on all sides. Remove them from the pan with a slotted spoon, drain on absorbent kitchen paper and place them on a serving dish. Pour over them the soya sauce, garnish with chopped spring onions and serve.

PREPARATION AND COOKING TIME 15 MINUTES

Pulses

Thai Curried Beancurd with Vegetables

SERVES 4

The vegetables listed in this recipe are only suggestions
and any suitable combination you have available may be
used. This curry, unlike most Thai curries, does not use
coconut milk and it is a little quicker and that much
simpler to prepare. Serve with rice

3 tablespoons vegetable oil
2 teaspoons curry powder
8 oz/225 g beancurd, pressed and cut into 1 in/2.5 cm cubes
1 teaspoon grated lemon rind *or* chopped lemon grass
4 oz/100 g green beans, cut into 2 in/5 cm lengths
4 oz/100 g cauliflower, cut into florets
4 oz/100 g cabbage *or* Chinese cabbage, coarsely shredded
4 oz/100 g fresh mushrooms, sliced
2 tablespoons soya sauce
2 teaspoons sugar

garnish

coriander *or* mint *or* parsley leaves, finely chopped

Heat the oil in a large pan or wok and stir fry the curry powder for 1–2
minutes. Add the beancurd and lemon rind and continue to stir fry for a
further 3–4 minutes. Add the green beans, cauliflower, cabbage,
mushrooms and soya sauce. Cook, stirring, until the vegetables are tender
enough to eat but still retain some 'bite' (about 4–5 minutes). Stir in the
sugar and serve garnished with fresh herbs.

PREPARATION AND COOKING TIME 25 MINUTES

Pulses

Dairy products are an important source of protein to a vegetarian – although not to vegans, who exclude them from their diets. They are also particularly convenient foods for the vegetarian who doesn't have a lot of time available for food preparation. At the same time, however, eggs, cheese, butter and, to a lesser extent, milk and yoghurt, are usually the main sources of saturated fats in a vegetarian diet. This is perfectly all right as long as these foods form only a moderate part of a varied diet of natural foods. If, however, dairy products contribute substantially to your diet, then it's a good idea to buy low fat cheeses, milk and yoghurt and to use polyunsaturated margarines (made if possible from cold-pressed oils) rather than butter.

The recipes given in this chapter have been chosen not only for their speed but for their nutritious ingredient combinations, colour and appearance. Most of them will stand on their own as a light meal or, served with a starter and/or soup and a dessert, as a substantial lunch or dinner

Egg, Cheese & Yoghurt Dishes

Chinese Eggs and Tomatoes
SERVES 4

6 eggs
1½ tablespoons rice wine *or* sherry
pinch salt
2 tablespoons vegetable oil

1¼ lb/550 g tomatoes, thickly sliced
4 tablespoons vegetable stock
garnish
2 spring onions, finely chopped

Beat the eggs with the rice wine and salt. Heat the oil in a frying pan. Fry the tomato slices over a moderate heat. Add a little salt and then the beaten egg mixture. Stir fry for 1–2 minutes, as for scrambled eggs. Pour in the stock and cook for a further minute. Serve immediately, very hot, sprinkled with the chopped spring onion.

PREPARATION AND COOKING TIME 15 MINUTES

Egg Bamboo
SERVES 2–4

This recipe illustrates the influence of Chinese cooking on Japanese cuisine. It is a fast recipe, useful for a quick, light meal

4 eggs
¼ teaspoon salt
¼ teaspoon freshly ground black pepper *or* togarashi
2 teaspoons rice vinegar *or* cider vinegar
4 oz/100 g canned bamboo shoots, cut into thin strips
2 tablespoons cooking oil
1 teaspoon soya sauce
½ teaspoon sugar
1 teaspoon sesame oil *or* other vegetable oil

garnish

1 spring onion, finely chopped

Beat the eggs in a bowl, add the salt, pepper and vinegar and mix in. Heat 1 tablespoon of oil in a wok or large frying pan and stir fry the bamboo shoots for 1 minute. Sprinkle with soya sauce and sugar, and fry for a further 30 seconds. Remove the bamboo shoots and oil from the pan. Heat another 1 tablespoon of oil in the wok and pour into it the egg mixture. Add the bamboo shoots and oil again, and stir together until the egg thickens. Stir in the sesame oil and serve garnished with spring onion.

PREPARATION AND COOKING TIME 15 MINUTES

Egg, Cheese & Yoghurt Dishes

Indonesian Omelette

SERVES 2–4

In this recipe all the omelette ingredients are combined and cooked together. The onion in it remains quite crunchy. If you wish, serve the omelette with the tomato sauce for which a recipe is given below. If you do this, make the sauce first. Both the omelette and the sauce contain chillies and they are hot!

2 tablespoons vegetable oil *or* 1 oz/25 g butter
1 small onion, finely sliced
1–2 fresh *or* dried red chillies, finely sliced
4 eggs, beaten
salt *and* pepper to taste

Combine all the ingredients except the oil and mix them well together. Heat a small or medium, heavy frying pan over a moderate heat, add half the oil, heat it and then add half the egg mixture. Cook until the omelette is set and lightly browned on the bottom side. Turn the omelette over and brown the other side. Repeat for the remaining half of the mixture.

Variation with chilli hot tomato sauce

1 tablespoon vegetable oil *or* butter
2 cloves garlic, crushed
1 small onion, diced
2 ripe tomatoes, chopped
1–2 fresh *or* dried red chillies, finely sliced
3 teaspoons dark soya sauce
2 tablespoons water
pepper to taste

Heat the oil in a small pan and sauté the onion and garlic until softened. Add the remaining ingredients and cook the mixture over a moderate heat until the tomatoes have disintegrated. Pour the sauce over the omelette and serve.

PREPARATION AND COOKING TIME 15 MINUTES
(WITH SAUCE ADD 10 MINUTES)

Egg, Cheese & Yoghurt Dishes

Spiced Egg and Yoghurt Salad

SERVES 4

This unusual dish looks plain to start with, but is transformed before serving by the addition of hot aromatic olive oil which is poured over the yoghurt

4 fresh eggs
¾ pint/450 ml natural yoghurt, chilled
salt *and* black pepper to taste
½ teaspoon dried mint
2 tablespoons olive oil
½ teaspoon cumin seeds, finely ground
½ teaspoon coriander seeds, finely ground
1 heaped teaspoon paprika

Soft boil the eggs, cool them a little under cold running water and shell them. Season the yoghurt to taste with salt and black pepper and divide it among 4 small individual plates. Place one egg in the centre of each plate and quarter it in rosette fashion. Place the plates before your guests. Put the olive oil in a small saucepan, add the cumin and coriander and bring the pan to a medium heat. Remove from the heat and stir in the paprika. Carry the pan to the table and pour some of the hot oil mixture over each egg and yoghurt salad.

PREPARATION AND COOKING TIME 20 MINUTES

Foo Yong Eggs and Cashew Nuts

SERVES 4–6

2 tablespoons vegetable oil
3 spring onions, finely chopped
1 clove garlic, crushed
1 in/2.5 cm piece root ginger, finely chopped
4 oz/100 g fresh mushrooms, sliced
2 oz/50 g canned bamboo shoots, diced
6 canned water chestnuts, chopped
6 oz/175 g cashew nuts
1 tablespoon dry sherry
salt
6 eggs, beaten

Egg, Cheese & Yoghurt Dishes

Heat the oil in a frying pan or wok, add the spring onion, garlic and ginger and stir fry for 1 minute. Add the mushrooms, bamboo shoots and water chestnuts and cook for a further 30 seconds. Stir in the nuts and sherry and season with salt. Lower the heat and pour in the beaten eggs. Scramble until the mixture is just set. Pile onto a warmed serving dish, garnish and serve.

PREPARATION AND COOKING TIME 20 MINUTES

Coriander Cream Eggs

SERVES 4

This dish makes an unusual change from, and is an improvement on, egg mayonnaise

4 fresh eggs
5 oz/150 ml coriander cream sauce (*see* p.72)
4 oz/100 g white mushrooms, stalks trimmed off
juice of ½ lemon
about 20 black olives

garnish

4 sprigs coriander

Boil the eggs quite hard. Meanwhile prepare the coriander cream sauce. Cool the eggs under running water, shell and quarter them. Take 4 plain white side plates and place a good heaped tablespoon of the green coriander sauce in the centre of each. Arrange the quartered eggs, yellow side up, around this. Finely slice the mushrooms and place them around the eggs. Dress the mushroom slices with lemon juice. Scatter the black olives over the plates and garnish the completed salad with the coriander sprigs.

PREPARATION AND COOKING TIME (INCLUDING SAUCE) 20 MINUTES

Egg, Cheese & Yoghurt Dishes

Buckwheat Omelette
SERVES 4

This recipe is from Japan where buckwheat is commonly used to make noodles. If buckwheat flour is unavailable you can use wholemeal flour

4 oz/100 g buckwheat flour
4 eggs, lightly beaten
4 fl oz/100 ml water
1 tablespoon soya sauce
1 small onion, diced
1 green pepper, seeded and diced
4 oz/100 g mushrooms, sliced
pepper to taste
2 tablespoons vegetable oil

Beat the flour, eggs, water and soya sauce into a smooth batter in a blender. Transfer to a mixing bowl and stir in all the remaining ingredients except the oil. Heat half the oil in a frying pan and ladle in half the batter mixture. Cook the omelette on both sides over a moderate heat until nicely browned. The vegetables should remain slightly crunchy in texture. Repeat for the remaining batter.

PREPARATION AND COOKING TIME 25 MINUTES

Piperade
SERVES 4

This is a colourful egg dish from the Basque region of France. It is quick to make and the ingredients are usually readily available. Be careful not to overcook the eggs. Serve the piperade with hot wholemeal toast

2 tablespoons vegetable oil (olive oil if possible)
1 lb/450 g onions, finely sliced
2 large red *or* green peppers, seeded and sliced
1 lb/450 g ripe tomatoes, chopped *or* tinned tomatoes, drained
salt *and* black pepper to taste
6 medium eggs, beaten

garnish
fresh basil, finely chopped *or* dried basil

Egg, Cheese & Yoghurt Dishes

Heat the oil over a moderate heat in a large frying pan that has a lid. Add the onions and cook, stirring, until just softened. Add the peppers and continue cooking and stirring until they are softened. Stir in the tomatoes and salt and black pepper to taste. Cover the pan and cook gently over a low heat for 7–8 minutes. The mixture should be moist rather than sloppy. If it's too wet, remove the lid of the pan and simmer off some of the liquid. Pour in the beaten eggs and stir continuously until the egg is lightly set, as you would cook scramble eggs. Sprinkle with basil and serve immediately.

PREPARATION AND COOKING TIME 25 MINUTES

Chatchouka (Eggs with Tomatoes)
SERVES 4

Chatchouka is a dish of North African origin. It was taken to Spain during the Arab invasion and is said to be the basis of the Spanish omelette. Chatchouka is popular throughout the Middle East

2 tablespoons vegetable oil
2 medium green peppers, seeded and thinly sliced
½–1 red chilli, finely chopped (optional)
2 medium onions, diced
2 cloves garlic, crushed
18 oz/500 g small tomatoes, halved
salt *and* black pepper to taste
6 medium eggs

garnish

fresh parsley, finely chopped

Heat the oil in a heavy or nonstick frying pan over a moderate heat and add the green peppers, chilli, onions and garlic. Stir fry until the onion is softened and lightly coloured. Add the tomatoes and cook gently, stirring occasionally, until they are very soft. Season to taste with salt and black pepper. Break the eggs over the surface of the contents of the frying pan and gently stir them with a wooden spoon to break the yolks. Cook, stirring occasionally, until the chatchouka is set. Serve garnished with parsley.

PREPARATION AND COOKING TIME 25 MINUTES

Egg, Cheese & Yoghurt Dishes

Potato, Walnut and Cottage Cheese Salad

SERVES 4–6

1 lb/450 g firm potatoes, scrubbed
2 medium firm tomatoes, quartered and then halved
1 small onion, finely diced
2 oz/50 g chopped walnuts
1 teaspoon dill seeds
2 tablespoons lemon juice
2 tablespoons olive oil *or* other vegetable oil
4 oz/100 g cottage cheese
2 oz/50 g natural low fat yoghurt
salt *and* black pepper to taste

garnish

fresh parsley *or* mint

Put the potatoes in their jackets into a pot. Cover with water and cook until just tender. Meanwhile prepare the other ingredients. Cool the potatoes under cold water, peel and thickly slice them. Combine the potatoes with the tomatoes, onion, walnuts and dill seeds. Beat together the lemon juice, oil, cottage cheese, yoghurt, and salt and pepper to taste, to form a smooth dressing. Pour this over the potato salad and gently stir it in. Garnish with parsley or mint and serve.

PREPARATION AND COOKING TIME 25 MINUTES
FREE TIME 10 MINUTES

Hot Cucumbers in Cheese Sauce with Almonds

SERVES 4

Cucumbers are nearly always served as a salad vegetable, but they are just as good hot on their own or with a sauce

1 oz/25 g butter
1 oz/25 g flour
8 fl oz/225 g hot milk
4 oz/100 g Cheddar cheese, grated
1 teaspoon prepared French mustard
salt *and* freshly milled black pepper to taste
2 medium cucumbers (1 lb/450 g approx) cut into 1 in/2.5 cm cubes, skins left on

garnish

4 oz/100 g almonds, lightly dry roasted

Egg, Cheese & Yoghurt Dishes

Set a medium pan of salted water to boil. Melt the butter in the top of a double boiler over boiling water and stir in the flour. Gradually stir in the hot milk and keep stirring until the sauce has thickened. Add the cheese slowly, and finally the mustard and seasoning. Leave the sauce simmering, stirring from time to time. Drop the cucumber cubes into the pan of boiling water and cook for 5 minutes only. Drain the cucumbers, tip them into the serving dish, pour the sauce over the top, top with roasted almonds and serve.

PREPARATION AND COOKING TIME 25 MINUTES

Cheese and Nut Balls

SERVES 4

Serve on their own or with a sauce (*see* pp.68–72) and spaghetti

2 tablespoons vegetable oil
1 medium onion, finely diced
2 cloves garlic, crushed
8 oz/225 g ground mixed nuts
8 oz/225 g wholemeal breadcrumbs
4 oz/100 g cheese, grated
2 teaspoons soya sauce
black pepper to taste
2 eggs, beaten

Preheat the oven to 375°F (190°C/gas mark 5). Sauté the onion and garlic in the oil until softened. Remove them from the heat and stir in the ground nuts and breadcrumbs. Combine the cheese, soya sauce, pepper and beaten eggs and mix well. Stir the nut and cheese mixtures together and mix thoroughly. With wet hands, form the mixture into 2 in/5 cm balls and place them on a greased baking sheet. Bake in the preheated oven for about 8 minutes or until brown and firm.

PREPARATION AND COOKING TIME 30 MINUTES
FREE TIME 10 MINUTES

Egg, Cheese & Yoghurt Dishes

Cottage Cheese, Fruit and Poppy Seed Salad

SERVES 4

8 oz/225 g cottage cheese
1 firm eating apple, cored and chopped
1 firm pear, cored and chopped
1 tablespoon roasted unsalted peanuts *or* other nuts
2 teaspoons poppy seeds
1 tablespoon lemon juice
1 teaspoon clear honey (optional)
salt *and* black pepper to taste

Combine all the ingredients, mix well and serve.

Variation with different fruit Other fresh fruit, depending on what is in season, may be used in this salad – for example, seedless green grapes, apricots, peaches, pineapple or melon.

PREPARATION TIME 15 MINUTES

Feta Cheese and Tomato Salad

SERVES 4–6

Feta cheese, which is made from sheep or goats' milk, is excellent with tomatoes and they are both delicious in a lemon and olive oil dressing, particularly if fresh basil is available as a flavouring. Serve with wholemeal bread for a simple light meal

1 small lettuce, leaves torn into bite-size pieces
6 oz/175 g feta cheese, cut into small pieces
3 firm medium tomatoes, chopped
2 oz/50 g black olives
2 tablespoons lemon juice
6 tablespoons olive oil
1 tablespoon fresh basil (optional)
salt *and* black pepper to taste

Place the lettuce leaves, feta cheese, tomatoes and olives in a salad bowl. Put the lemon juice, olive oil, basil, salt and black pepper to taste in a blender, and blend until smooth. Pour the dressing over the salad, toss well and serve.

PREPARATION TIME 15 MINUTES

Egg, Cheese & Yoghurt Dishes

For that special occasion Tropical Fruit Salad and Strawberry Cream Sorbet
make an irresistable combination

Fresh fruits are nature's most obvious desserts. Fresh Fruit Compote is the perfect end to a meal or, for an occasional treat, serve honey-glazed Deep-fried Bananas

Peanut Cheeseburgers

MAKES 4 LARGE BURGERS

1 tablespoon vegetable oil
½ medium onion, finely diced
2 oz/50 g mushrooms, sliced
4 oz/100 g peanuts, coarsely ground *or*
4 oz/100 g crunchy peanut butter
2 oz/50 g sesame seeds, lightly dry roasted
2 tablespoons tahini

juice of 1 lemon
2 oz/50 g wholemeal breadcrumbs
4 oz/100 g Cheddar cheese, grated
salt *and* black pepper to taste
1 egg, beaten
wholemeal flour for coating
oil for shallow frying

Sauté the onion in oil until softened. Add the mushrooms and sauté for a further minute. Combine this mixture with the peanuts, sesame seeds, tahini, lemon juice, breadcrumbs, cheese, and salt and pepper to taste. Stir well and mix thoroughly. Add a little flour if the mixture is too moist. Press the mixture into 4 burger shapes, brush them with beaten egg and coat them with a light sprinkling of wholemeal flour. Fry nicely brown on both sides and serve.

PREPARATION AND COOKING TIME 20 MINUTES

Baked Tomatoes with Walnut and Cottage Cheese Filling

SERVES 4

4 large firm tomatoes
salt *and* black pepper to taste
4 oz/100 g cottage cheese
2 oz/50 g chopped walnuts

2 oz/50 g wholemeal breadcrumbs
1 tablespoon freshly diced onion
½ teaspoon dried thyme
1 tablespoon vegetable oil

Preheat the oven to 375° F (190° C/gas mark 5). Cut ½ in/1.25 cm tops off the tomatoes and scoop out the inside, leaving ½ in/1.25 cm shell. Sprinkle the inside of each shell with a little of the salt and black pepper. Combine the cottage cheese, walnuts, breadcrumbs, onion, thyme, salt and black pepper and mix well. Stuff the tomatoes with the mixture and press the tops back into place. Brush the tomatoes with oil and put them on a greased baking sheet. Bake for 20 minutes.

PREPARATION AND COOKING TIME 30 MINUTES
FREE TIME 15 MINUTES

Egg, Cheese & Yoghurt Dishes

Tortillas with Cheese Filling

SERVES 4

4 tablespoons vegetable oil *or* butter
1 medium onion, finely diced
1 lb/450 g Cheddar cheese, grated
2 tablespoons finely chopped parsley

¼ teaspoon chilli powder
¼ teaspoon ground cumin
salt *and* black pepper to taste
8 wholemeal tortillas (shop-bought)

Preheat the oven to 400°F (200°C/gas mark 6). Sauté the onion in half the oil until softened. Combine the cheese, parsley, chilli powder, cumin and seasoning with the onion and the oil it was cooked in. Mix well. Place a line of filling down each tortilla and then fold them over firmly. Place the stuffed tortillas on a greased baking dish and brush the tops with the remaining oil. Now bake them, uncovered, for 15 minutes or cover them with tomato sauce and bake for 20 minutes.

PREPARATION AND COOKING TIME 30 MINUTES
FREE TIME 10 MINUTES

Cheese Rice Cakes

SERVES 4

6 oz/175 g short grain white rice
4 oz/100 g cheese, finely grated
4 oz/100 g cottage cheese
1 small onion, finely diced
2 eggs beaten
1 tablespoon wholemeal flour

¼ teaspoon nutmeg
½ teaspoon cinnamon
salt *and* pepper to taste
wholemeal breadcrumbs or
flour for coating
oil for shallow frying

Cook the rice in plenty of boiling water. As soon as it is tender, drain and rinse under cold water. Meanwhile, combine the cheeses, onion and half the beaten egg in a mixing bowl and stir well together. Add the flour, nutmeg, cinnamon, and salt and pepper to taste. Mix well by hand. Mix in the drained rice and add more flour, slowly, if the mixture is not firm enough to hold its shape. With wet hands, shape the mixture into about 10 round cakes. Dip the rice cakes into the remaining beaten egg and roll them in breadcrumbs or flour. Heat the oil in a frying pan and gently fry the rice cakes until nicely browned on both sides (about 5 minutes each side). Keep cooked cakes warm under a low grill while frying the remainder.

PREPARATION AND COOKING TIME 30 MINUTES

Egg, Cheese & Yoghurt Dishes

Fruit and Vegetable Yoghurt Salad

SERVES 4–6

2 medium eating apples, cored and chopped
2 medium carrots, peeled and thinly sliced
1 medium green pepper, seeded and chopped
6 oz/175 g fresh *or* tinned pineapple pieces
6 fl oz/175 ml natural yoghurt
3 tablespoons orange juice
1 tablespoon lemon juice
pinch salt

garnish

cinnamon

Combine the apples, carrots, pepper and pineapple and mix well. Stir together the yoghurt, orange and lemon juices and salt. Toss the salad in this dressing, and serve with cinnamon dusted over the top.

PREPARATION TIME 15 MINUTES

Spinach, Walnut and Yoghurt Salad

SERVES 4

1 lb/450 g spinach, washed and chopped *or* 8 oz/225 g frozen spinach,
defrosted and drained
1 medium onion, finely diced
1 tablespoon olive oil
8 fl oz/225 ml natural low fat yoghurt
1 clove garlic, finely chopped
2 tablespoons chopped walnuts

garnish

1 teaspoon crushed dried mint

Put the spinach and onion in a heavy pan. Cover and cook gently with no added water, until the spinach is wilted and soft (about 7 minutes). Add the oil to the pan and cook for a further 5 minutes. Combine the yoghurt and garlic and lightly dry toast the walnuts. Transfer the spinach and onions to a serving bowl, pour the yoghurt over them, sprinkle the walnuts on top, garnish with crushed mint and serve.

PREPARATION AND COOKING TIME 25 MINUTES
FREE TIME 10 MINUTES

Egg, Cheese & Yoghurt Dishes

Ginger and Yoghurt Rice Salad

SERVES 4

8 oz/225 g long grain white rice, washed and drained
2 in/5 cm piece fresh root ginger, peeled and finely chopped
8 fl oz/225 ml low fat natural yoghurt
1 medium green pepper, seeded and finely chopped
1 stalk celery, chopped
2 oz/50 g roasted peanuts
salt to taste
cayenne to taste (optional)

Cook the rice in plenty of boiling water until tender. Drain, and rinse well under cold water until cooled. Set aside to drain again, and prepare the other ingredients. Combine them with the rice, mix well and serve.

PREPARATION AND COOKING TIME 25 MINUTES
FREE TIME 10 MINUTES

Spiced Vegetables in Yoghurt

SERVES 4

2 tablespoons vegetable oil
2 medium onions, chopped
2 medium green peppers, seeded and chopped
2 medium carrots, cut into matchsticks
2 sticks celery, chopped
½ red fresh *or* dried chilli, seeded and chopped *or* ¼ teaspoon hot chilli sauce
½ teaspoon ground cumin
½ teaspoon turmeric
½ teaspoon ground coriander
salt *and* black pepper to taste
½ pint/275 ml natural low fat yoghurt

Heat the oil in a pan and add the onion, green peppers, carrots and celery. Sauté, stirring, over a medium heat until the onion has started to brown and the other vegetables are still a little crunchy. Reduce the heat and stir in the chilli, cumin, turmeric, coriander, and salt and black pepper to taste. Cover the pan and cook, stirring occasionally, for 5 minutes. Stir in the yoghurt and cook, uncovered, for a further 5 minutes. The contents should not boil once the yoghurt has been added.

PREPARATION AND COOKING TIME 25 MINUTES

Egg, Cheese & Yoghurt Dishes

$\mathcal{F}$resh fruits are nature's most obvious desserts and snack foods. They need no preparation, they refresh the palate and they contribute valuable nutrients to the diet. Fruit in season is usually the tastiest and cheapest. Nowadays the skin on fruit, especially apples, may be contaminated with pesticides or wax so it is most important to wash it well before eating. Dried fruits are also a very useful ingredient in the vegetarian diet. As long as you remember to pre-soak those that need it, dried fruits are an excellent, ready-to-use ingredient in breakfast cereals, fruit salads, and sweet and savoury dishes.

The fruit desserts chosen for this chapter were picked for their speed, convenience of preparation, versatility and healthiness. With two or three exceptions they are also low in sugar and fat content. Bananas are a major ingredient in four of the recipes. I included so many because bananas are available all year round, they are nutritionally good, and because I like them, particularly deep fried in batter as an occasional treat!

Incidentally, raw fruit and vegetable juices freshly made in your own juicer are an excellent way of obtaining the nutrients of fruits and vegetables in a quick, convenient and concentrated form

Fruit Desserts

Healthy Banana Delight

SERVES 4

2 large bananas, sliced
1 tablespoon wheatgerm
1 tablespoon ground almonds
2 tablespoons milk
juice of 1 orange
1 tablespoon concentrated apple juice

Put all the ingredients into a liquidizer and blend for about 30 seconds.
Distribute among 4 fruit bowls and serve.

PREPARATION TIME 5 MINUTES

Strawberry Cream Sorbet

SERVES 2–4

This recipe is for strawberry sorbet, but any frozen fruit is suitable

4 fl oz/100 ml whipping cream
8 oz/225 g frozen strawberries
2 tablespoons honey *or* maple syrup

Whip the cream very stiff and return it to the refrigerator. Put the strawberries and honey into a blender. Pulse the machine until the mixture is smooth. Transfer it to a serving bowl and fold in the whipped cream. Serve immediately, or store in the freezer part of the refrigerator until needed.

PREPARATION TIME 10 MINUTES

Rose-flavoured Apples

SERVES 4

This dessert is refreshing and cooling on a hot summer's day

1 lb/450 g eating apples, cored
juice of 1 lemon
2 oz/50 g caster sugar

2 tablespoons rose water
cinnamon
crushed ice

Grate the apples into a mixing bowl and stir in the lemon juice, sugar and rose water. Transfer to individual serving bowls, dust with a little cinnamon and top with crushed ice. Serve.

PREPARATION TIME 10 MINUTES

Fruit Desserts

Fruit Salad with Preserved Ginger

SERVES 4

1 dessert apple, chopped
1 ripe pear, chopped
1 banana, sliced
1 peach *or* other soft fruit, chopped
1 dessertspoon preserved ginger, chopped
1 oz/25 g raisins, washed
1 tablespoon concentrated apple juice (optional)
4 fl oz/100 ml orange juice
2 teaspoons of the ginger syrup from the preserved ginger jar

Mix together in a serving bowl the apple, pear, banana, peach, ginger and raisins. Whisk together the apple juice, orange juice and ginger syrup, pour this sauce over the fruit and serve immediately.

PREPARATION TIME 15 MINUTES

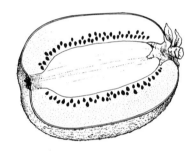

Tropical Fruit Salad

SERVES 4

½ ripe pineapple, peeled, cored and chopped
1 banana, sliced
2 kiwi fruits, halved and sliced
1 mango, peeled and chopped
1 tablespoon lemon juice
5 fl oz/150 ml grape juice

Mix together the pineapple, banana, kiwi fruits and mango. Pour the lemon and grape juices over the fruit and serve immediately.

PREPARATION TIME 15 MINUTES

Fruit Desserts

Uncooked Fruit Nut Balls

MAKES 16

8 oz/225 g finely chopped walnuts
8 oz/225 g finely chopped figs
8 oz/225 g finely chopped dates
8 oz/225 g raisins
1 tablespoon fresh orange juice
1 teaspoon grated orange peel *or* lemon peel

garnish

16 whole walnuts

Combine all the ingredients and knead into a consistent mixture. Pinch off small amounts and form into small balls. Top each with a whole walnut.

PREPARATION TIME 15 MINUTES

Banana Pancakes

SERVES 4

2 eggs, beaten
½ teaspoon salt
4 oz/100 g wholemeal flour
½ pint/275 ml milk
1 tablespoon brown sugar *or* honey
2 medium bananas, peeled and mashed
vegetable oil for frying
lemon juice to taste

To prepare the batter, combine all the ingredients except the oil and lemon juice in a blender and beat smooth. Brush a heavy frying pan with a little oil and heat it over a moderate flame. Pour some batter into the pan and swirl it around to form a thin ¼ in/6 mm coating on the surface of the pan. Lightly brown the bottom side of the pancake, and then turn it over and brown the other side. Repeat for the remaining batter, pile the cooked pancakes on top of one another on a buttered plate, then serve them sprinkled with lemon juice.

PREPARATION AND COOKING TIME 15 MINUTES

Fruit Desserts

Uncooked Date and Yoghurt Stuffed Apples

SERVES 4

4 sweet, firm apples, cored
juice of 1 lemon
2 oz/50 g whole fresh dates
1 oz/25 g raisins
4 fl oz/100 ml natural yoghurt
2 teaspoons rose water
2 teaspoons brown sugar
¼ teaspoon ground cardamom
¼ teaspoon ground cinnamon
2 oz/50 g pistachio nuts

Put the apples in a bowl, cover them in water, add the lemon juice to the water and set aside. Stone the dates, set 4 aside and finely chop the rest. Add the raisins, yoghurt, rose water, sugar, cardamom and cinnamon to the chopped dates and mix well. Stuff each of the reserved whole dates with a pistachio and crush the remaining pistachios. Drain the apples and stuff them with the yoghurt mixture. Top each one with a pistachio-stuffed date and sprinkle with crushed pistachios.

PREPARATION TIME 15 MINUTES

Shallow Fried Bananas

SERVES 4

Bananas of many varieties are abundant in South East Asia. They are popular fried and deep fried, both as street snacks and as desserts at home

2 tablespoons peanut oil *or* butter
4 firm bananas, peeled, sliced lengthwise and then crosswise to give 4 pieces per banana
3 tablespoons brown *or* white sugar, according to taste
lemon juice *or* lime juice to taste

Heat the oil in a wok or frying pan. Add the banana pieces and fry them on both sides over a moderate heat until very lightly browned. Spoon the sugar over the top and gently stir it in until it dissolves. Transfer the bananas and sugar syrup to serving dishes, sprinkle with lemon juice and serve.

PREPARATION AND COOKING TIME 15 MINUTES

Fruit Desserts

Deep Fried Bananas

SERVES 4

5 fl oz/125 ml water
5 oz/125 g rice flour *or* plain white flour
1 egg, beaten
2 tablespoons desiccated coconut
pinch salt
4 firm bananas, peeled, sliced lengthwise and then crosswise to give
4 pieces per banana
oil for deep frying

Combine the water, flour, egg, coconut and salt in a mixing bowl and whisk into a smooth batter. Heat the oil for deep frying until it just starts to smoke. Dip the banana slices in the batter and fry them 5–6 at a time until golden brown and crispy. Remove them with a slotted spoon and drain on a paper towel before serving. Repeat for all the banana pieces.

PREPARATION AND COOKING TIME 20 MINUTES

Apple, Banana and Lemon Dessert

SERVES 4

Serve with natural yoghurt, garnished with toasted almonds

8 oz/225 g sugar
8 fl oz/225 ml water
4 tart apples, peeled, cored and sliced
2 bananas, peeled and sliced
rind of 2 lemons, grated
juice of 2 lemons
2 teaspoons ground cinnamon

Put the sugar and water into a heavy pan and bring to the boil. Add the apples, bananas, lemon rind, lemon juice and cinnamon. Simmer until nearly all the liquid has evaporated and the mixture has thickened (about 15 minutes). Serve hot or cold.

PREPARATION AND COOKING TIME 25 MINUTES
FREE TIME 15 MINUTES

Fruit Desserts

Baked Ginger and Citrus Bananas

SERVES 4

2 oz/50 g butter
2 oz/50 g white sugar
1 tablespoon lemon juice
1 tablespoon orange juice
½ teaspoon cinnamon
1 teaspoon grated lemon rind
2 teaspoons finely chopped root ginger
4 bananas, peeled and cut in half crosswise

Preheat the oven to 375°F (190°C/gas mark 5). Beat together the butter and sugar and then beat in all the remaining ingredients except the bananas. Lightly grease a shallow baking dish and arrange the banana pieces on the bottom. Pour over the butter/ginger mixture and bake for 15 minutes. Serve immediately.

PREPARATION AND COOKING TIME 25 MINUTES
FREE TIME 15 MINUTES

Winter Fruit Medley

SERVES 2–4

This is good as a dessert or a winter breakfast starter. It is especially tasty in late winter and early spring when the first unforced rhubarb is available

2 oz/50 g dried prunes, soaked, stoned and chopped
2 oz/50 g dried apricots, soaked and chopped
1 oz/25 g sultanas
2 sticks rhubarb, chopped
1 teaspoon lemon juice
1 cooking apple, cored and chopped
honey to taste

garnish

creamed coconut, flaked

Put all the ingredients in a saucepan except for the coconut. Cover with water and cook for 20 minutes. Serve hot or cold, with honey to taste, topped with flakes of creamed coconut.

PREPARATION AND COOKING TIME 30 MINUTES
FREE TIME 15 MINUTES

Fruit Desserts

Fruit-topped Uncooked Nut Cake

MAKES 1 LB/450 G CAKE

8 oz/225 g oatflakes
4 oz/100 g nuts, finely chopped
1 large banana, mashed
1 medium carrot, grated
juice of 1 lemon

1 tablespoon brown sugar
2 tablespoons treacle
water *or* milk *or* cream
fresh fruit in season *or*
tinned fruit, drained

Combine all the ingredients except the water and fruit and mix well. Add enough water to form the mixture into a moist, sticky consistency. Press the mixture into a round, shallow cake tin and decorate the top with fruit pieces. Put it in the freezer section of the refrigerator for 15 minutes and then serve with fresh cream.

PREPARATION AND CHILLING TIME 30 MINUTES
FREE TIME 15 MINUTES

Fresh Fruit Compote

SERVES 4

4 oz/100 g sugar
12 fl oz/350 ml water
2 peaches, skinned
2 tart apples, washed
8 oz/225 g plums, washed, stoned and halved
8 oz/225 g strawberries, washed
2 sticks cinnamon *or* 1 teaspoon ground cinnamon
juice of 1 lemon

Put the sugar and water in a pan and bring to the boil. Set to simmer. Slice the skinned peaches and the apples and put them into the simmering syrup. Add the plums, strawberries, cinnamon and lemon juice. Simmer for 15 minutes, stirring occasionally. Remove the cinnamon sticks (if used). Serve hot or cold with whipped cream or natural yoghurt.

Variation with rose water If rose water is available add 1–2 drops to the simmering fruit.

Variation with cardamom Try cardamom in place of the cinnamon for a different flavour.

PREPARATION AND COOKING TIME 30 MINUTES
FREE TIME 15 MINUTES

Fruit Desserts

WEIGHTS AND MEASURES

Imperial/metric

Weights

Imperial	Approximate metric equivalent
½ oz	15 g
1 oz	25 g
2 oz	50 g
3 oz	75 g
4 oz	100 g
5 oz	150 g
6 oz	175 g
7 oz	200 g
8 oz	225 g
9 oz	250 g
10 oz	275 g
11 oz	300 g
12 oz	350 g
13 oz	375 g
14 oz	400 g
15 oz	425 g
1 lb	450 g
2 lb	900 g
3 lb	1.4 kg

Exact conversion: 1 oz = 28.35 g

Liquids

Imperial	Approximate metric equivalent
¼ teaspoon	1.25 ml
½ teaspoon	2.5 ml
1 teaspoon	5 ml
2 teaspoons	10 ml
1 tablespoon	15 ml
2 tablespoons	30 ml
3 tablespoons	45 ml
1 fl oz	25 ml
2 fl oz	50 ml
3 fl oz	75 ml
4 fl oz	100 ml
5 fl oz (¼ pint)	150 ml
6 fl oz	175 ml
7 fl oz	200 ml
8 fl oz	225 ml
9 fl oz	250 ml
10 fl oz (½ pint)	275 ml
15 fl oz (¾ pint)	450 ml
20 fl oz (1 pint)	550 ml
1¾ pints	1 litre
2 pints	1.1 litres

Oven temperatures

°F	°C	Gas mark
225	110	¼
250	130	½
275	140	1
300	150	2
325	170	3
350	180	4
375	190	5
400	200	6
425	220	7
450	230	8
475	240	9

American Can Weights

8 oz can	= 8 oz	= 1 cup
Picnic	= 10½ to 12 oz	= 1¼ cups
12 oz can	= 12 oz	= 1½ cups
No. 300 can	= 14–16 oz	= 1¾ cups
No. 303 can	= 16–17 oz	= 2 cups
No. 2 can	= 1 lb 4 oz or 20 oz	= 2½ cups
No. 2½ can	= 1 lb 13 oz or 29 oz	= 3½ cups
No. 3 can	= 2 lb 14 oz or 1 quart 14 fluid oz	= 5¾ cups

British and American equivalents

This book was written for a British readership. To help the American cook with the system of measurement used, here is a conversion table showing imperial weights with their American cup equivalent.

British	American	British	American
8 fl oz	1 cup	3½ oz cumin seeds	1 cup
½ pint/10 fl oz	1¼ cups	8 oz cooking dates	1 cup
16 fl oz	1 pint	4½ oz wholewheat flour	1 cup
1 pint/20 fl oz	2½ cups	4 oz white flour	1 cup
2 pints/40 fl oz	2½ pints = 5 cups	4 oz green beans, chopped	1 cup
		7 oz dried lentils	1 cup
2 tablespoons	⅛ cup/ 1½ table-spoons	7 oz cooked lentils	1 cup
		3½ oz mangetout	1 cup
8 tablespoons	½ cup	9 oz miso (Japanese soya bean paste)	1 cup
4 oz ground almonds	1 cup	2 oz broken noodles	1 cup
5 oz almonds, unblanched	1 cup	6 oz diced onion	1 cup
4½ oz dried apricots	1 cup	2 oz parsley, finely chopped	1 cup
7 oz aubergines, diced	1 cup	6 oz peanut butter	1 cup
6 oz bamboo shoots, drained and sliced	1 cup	5 oz peanuts	1 cup
4 oz beancurd, drained	1 cup	3½ oz black peppercorns	1 cup
6 oz beans (canned)	1 cup	6 oz canned pineapple chunks, drained	1 cup
3 oz beansprouts	1 cup	6 oz raisins or sultanas	1 cup
3½ oz broccoli (fresh), sliced	1 cup	8 oz dry rice (brown or white)	1¼ cups
4 oz bulgar wheat	1 cup	6 oz sesame seeds	1 cup
4 oz butter	1 stick	8 oz cooked spinach	1¼ cups
8 oz butter	1 cup	1 lb raw spinach	5 cups
4 oz cabbage, shredded, firmly packed	1 cup	6½ oz cooked red beans	1 cup
4 oz cauliflower, in florets	1 cup	8 oz granulated sugar	1 cup
4 oz cheese, grated	1 cup	6 oz brown sugar	1 cup
4 oz cooked chick peas	1 cup	9 oz canned tomatoes	1 cup
2 oz flaked, unsweetened coconut	1 cup	8 oz tomatoes	2 medium tomatoes
3½ oz coriander seeds	1 cup	9 oz tomato paste	1 cup
4 oz sweetcorn kernels	1 cup	7 oz vegetable fat	1 cup
6 oz cornflour	1 cup	4 oz walnuts, chopped	1 cup
5 oz courgettes, sliced	1 cup	6½ oz water chestnuts, drained	1 cup
		1 oz yeast	½ cup

INDEX